STARTUP TO IPO

STARTUP TO IPO

How to Build and Finance a Technology Company

Donald H. MacAdam

To order additional copies of this book, contact:
Xlibris Corporation
1-888-795-4274
www.Xlibris.com
Orders@Xlibris.com
22478

CONTENTS

The helpful comments and suggestions of
John Simard, Cam Goodnough, John Sinton and Fred
Peters, and many years of honest advice from
Tim Snelgrove, made this book possible.
Thanks.
For everything else, I thank Diane.

.

CHAPTER ONE

The Entrepreneur

"And so each venture is a new beginning."
T. S. Eliot

The first guru of the microcomputer age was born in Thailand, raised in India and educated in the United Kingdom. Through hard work, incredible communication skills and blind luck, Adam Osborne, the son of an expatriate British philosopher, changed the world. Adam was a chemical engineer by training, but when Shell Oil relocated from the San Francisco area to Texas in 1970, he abruptly became an unemployed chemical engineer. With the petrochemical industry in a slump and jobs scarce, Adam was forced into the traditional role of the highly trained and unemployed: he became a consultant. Some of his early jobs involved technical writing for clients in the semiconductor industry including microcomputer documentation for Intel Corporation, National Semiconductor and Fairchild Semiconductor.

In 1972, the microcomputer revolution had not yet been born, but seeing it coming, Adam formed Osborne and Associates to write easy-to-understand manuals on the subject. He offered to sell his first book, *An Introduction to Microprocessors*, to his clients but was turned down. Next, he submitted the manuscript to publishers with the same result. So, in typical entrepreneurial fashion, he published the book himself. By 1977, *An Introduction to Microprocessors* was the highest selling commercial textbook in the world. Adam promoted his books in a series of lecture tours where, in addition to an education, tens of thousands of engineers and technicians received a witty and controversial look inside Silicon

Valley. Typical quote: "I define a 'feature' as an error in design that engineering could not eliminate in time so they gave it to marketing to take care of." Another: "Adequacy is sufficient." By the time he sold his publishing company to McGraw-Hill in 1979, more than thirty titles, many written by Adam himself, had been published.

In addition to books, Adam also wrote a column "From the Fountainhead" that appeared in *Interface Age* and *InfoWorld*. From his media pulpit, Adam pontificated on the sad state of affairs in the computer industry. A recurrent theme was the lack of innovation in an industry where companies manufactured only hardware or only software while what the customer needed was a computer system. In addition, prices were too high and bulky computers only met the needs of desk-bound workers in office cubicles. Adam foresaw that low cost, portable and easy-to-use computer systems were the future and, more to the point, he decided to do something about it.

With the money from the sale of his publishing business, Adam set out to convert his vision into reality. He drafted a specification for an entirely new concept in computing: a fully functional portable system that came complete with software. Like Henry Ford and his Model T, there would be no options available for Adam's new computer, but there would also be no need for options. It would come fully loaded. The packaged software would include a word processor for composing documents, a spreadsheet program for crunching numbers, and a BASIC interpreter for everything else. There would be 64K of random access memory, a keyboard and numeric keypad, a 5" monitor, two floppy disk drives, a serial and a parallel interface, a separate modem interface, a connection for an external video monitor, and a connection for an external battery pack. The complete system would be small enough to fit under an airline seat and, most importantly, the Osborne 1 would be priced at $1,795, less than half the price of an equivalent computer system.

Specification in hand, Adam convinced Lee Felsenstein, a technical wizard, and Jack Melchor, a prominent venture capitalist, to join him. The three men founded Osborne Computer Corporation and, months before the product's technical design was completed, Adam pre-announced the Osborne 1 in the spring of 1981 at the West Coast Computer Fair. It was a proven marketing strategy, borrowed from the semiconductor industry, in which a new product is widely publicized in advance of its commercial introduction. Pre-marketing the Osborne 1 was good for Osborne Computer, which built a sizable backlog including prepaid orders, and bad for its competitors, who saw an immediate drop in demand from customers who were willing to postpone their purchases until the more powerful and less costly computer system was available. In spite of detractors who labelled the 23-pound portable computer as "luggable," by the time the Osborne 1 began shipping there was an enormous pent-up demand.

Six months after launch, Osborne Computer had its first million dollar sales month. In the company's second year of operations when sales reached $68 million, a number of competitors emerged with products to compete with the Osborne 1. But there was no catching Adam, he had coined the term "hypergrowth" and he was its ablest practitioner. In the spring of 1983, a mere two years after the Osborne 1 was introduced to the world, the company was riding a tidal wave of sales and ten thousand units were shipped in a single month. Also in the spring of 1983, the design of Osborne's next generation computer was completed and scheduled to enter production in a few months. "Executive" retained the popular features of the Osborne 1 such as portability, packaged software, and low cost, yet was significantly more powerful. With its established position in the market and its next generation product to be available soon, industry watchers expected another year of hypergrowth for Osborne Computer.

The strategy of pre-marketing, which had been enormously successful in the case of the Osborne 1, was now used to introduce Executive and it had exactly the same effect. Once again, customers clamoured to place advance orders for Executive and cancelled or postponed ordering from the competition, but a serious miscalculation became immediately apparent. This time Osborne Computer was competing with itself. With a superior model soon to be available, new orders for the Osborne 1 dried up. N shipments plunged from ten thousand units to practically nothing and the momentum of a company that had experienced 24 months of hypergrowth now spawned a hypergrowth of red ink. The fast-paced downhill slide was unstoppable and within a few months Osborne Computer Corporation filed for bankruptcy.

The lesson of the Osborne Computer story is clear: a company must carefully plan the introduction of a new product that obsoletes an old product. But the tale also conveys a wider meaning and a sobering message, namely companies are fragile entities that can be brought down by a single error.

Adam and I were business associates for ten years. My company, Varah Electronics, sold the first of his books and the last of his computers. The final time I saw Adam was less than a year after the collapse of Osborne Computer. We had dinner at a floating restaurant in Sausalito with a stunning view of the San Francisco skyline. We ate Italian shellfish stew and drank cabernet sauvignon. Adam was in high spirits. He had recently purchased a new sailboat and intended to one day sail it around the world. But that adventure would have to wait a little longer. Over espresso, Adam announced his intention to change the computer industry one more time. His new company, Paperback Software International, planned to meet the needs of a burgeoning mass market by selling low cost software through bookstores.

But it was not to be. While the new company flourished for a few years, Paperback Software was sued in 1987 for infringement. Intimidated by a lawsuit brought by the then-mighty Lotus Development Corporation, bookstores began to pull Paperback Software's products off the shelves. Sales dropped precipitously and in 1990, a month after the case went to court, Adam resigned from the company. Two years later, in an association with an Indian computer company, Adam founded Noetics Software to commercialize neural networks and fuzzy logic. Adam believed these new technologies that mimic human thought processes would profoundly change the computer business. It would be his third big chance. However, after the initial publicity, the venture fizzled out and nothing more was heard about Noetics Software or its founder. The best-known and most articulate critic of the computer establishment had vanished from sight. For more than a decade, while the Osborne 1 found its way into the collection of the Smithsonian Institution and its legacy matured into the ubiquitous laptop computer, the whereabouts of Adam Osborne were unknown. The mystery of his fate was sadly resolved in March 2003. Adam died in his sleep at the age of 64 in Kodiakanal, a small village in southern India, where he had endured a ten-year battle with brain disease.

The defining characteristic of Adam Osborne, who found nothing more satisfying than starting and building a company, was his entrepreneurial spirit. If new companies are an essential part of a healthy economy, and I believe they are, then so too are entrepreneurs. This book is for them.

CHAPTER TWO

Intellectual Property

"Efficiency is intelligent laziness."
Linda Petruzzelli

A cable tie is a plastic strip with a head and a tail. The head has a slot with a locking mechanism, and the tail is tapered to fit into the slot. In the application for which it was originally designed, an assembler wraps the cable tie around a bundle of wires, inserts the tail into the head, and cinches it tight. In this role of keeping current-carrying wires in their place, the cable tie fulfills a basic safety requirement of electrical equipment. However, when Thomas & Betts Corporation introduced its patented cable tie in the 1960s, there was an alternative product that served the same purpose and was much less expensive: twine.

On the surface, a new product that is much more expensive than the product it is intended to replace, appears to be a bad idea. However, Thomas & Betts had the good sense to look at the competitive issue from a broader perspective. A low-cost unskilled worker could install cable ties faster than a higher-cost skilled worker could secure bundles of wire with twine. The reduction in labor cost more than offset the difference in price. In addition, products assembled with twine were variable in quality while products assembled with cable ties were consistent in quality. Cable ties became a fast-growing business and Thomas & Betts had a patented monopoly. In the absence of competitive pricing pressures, the profits rolled in and volumes grew at an astounding pace.

Unfortunately, from the point of view of Thomas & Betts, a

company by the name of Panduit Corporation found a way around the patent. The Thomas & Betts patent utilized a small piece of barbed metal in the head of the tie as the locking device. Panduit figured out how to make the entire cable tie, including the locking device, out of a single piece of plastic. This "one-piece" cable tie not only performed as well as the product from Thomas & Betts, but also was less expensive to manufacture. With a significant cost advantage in favor of the competition, Thomas & Betts braced themselves for a long and drawn out price war. In the technology industry, it is not uncommon for a once-profitable business to be decimated by rampant price competition. However, in this case there was no price war.

In spite of the cost advantage, Panduit did not go after the market on the basis of price. Instead, Panduit set their prices in line with Thomas & Betts and marketed their one-piece cable tie as more reliable. Customers were told that the Panduit cable tie, without the little metal barb that was integral to its competitor's design, eliminated the possibility of tiny metal pieces dropping onto and shorting out expensive equipment. The argument was not strong enough to win the war against an entrenched and much larger competitor, but was sufficiently persuasive to win many battles and gradually gain market share. And, since Panduit had the good sense not to sell at a lower price in spite of their lower cost, every sale must have generated lots of cash.

I use the words, "must have generated" because, unlike most large companies, Panduit Corporation is private. Its financial information is not publicly available. I know a bit about the company because Varah Electronics was one of its authorized distributors. The guiding principal of Panduit management was to sell high quality products at prices that were usually a notch higher than the competition. There were constant pressures from the sales force to lower prices, but Panduit management held to the high margin strategy. At the time, it seemed to me that Panduit was in a position to dominate the market because their costs were lower than the competition. I did not understand why they refused to take the low margin business. Because of their policies, I lost sales. I remember thinking Panduit management were obtuse. I now understand I used the incorrect word. They were smart.

The strategy of Panduit ran counter to the prevailing wisdom of the eighties and nineties that the best strategy is one leading to market domination. But Panduit's management was right and the conventional wisdom was wrong. For example, the pursuit of market dominance through acquisitions and price wars has devastated the telecom, fiber optic, cell phone, wireless equipment, data equipment, and security software industries. Some companies, for example Intel and Microsoft, have been successful and also dominate their markets, but the success of their sales and technology strategies led to their market dominance, not the other way around. In itself, market dominance is a poor strategy. The best business strategy is one leading to the success of the enterprise, with success defined in terms of sustained profitability. Not only does a company have to make money today, it also has to make money tomorrow. A company with profitability as a goal is far better positioned than a company whose principal goal is size.

It is on this basis that Panduit has been run. Company management understood it was better to control one-third of a profitable market than two-thirds of an unprofitable market. Thanks to its profits, Panduit has been able to expand its business into a wide range of lucrative niche markets. To the cable television industry, Panduit sells cable ties made out of a special plastic that does not become brittle in the sunshine and therefore lasts longer; to the telecommunications industry, Panduit sells color-coded and pre-numbered cable ties that simplify maintenance and lead to higher service levels and lower costs; and, to the consumer products industry, Panduit sells cable ties that are dispensed by automatic equipment at the lowest possible installed cost. These cable tie products, and a number of additional product lines that have been introduced over the years, have been compatible with Panduit's manufacturing capabilities, their sales organization and the company's investment in intellectual property. Always taking the high road, always a quality rather than a price leader, the owners of Panduit have built a $400 million business with 3,500 employees, and are an excellent example of how to build a profitable and sustainable private company. However, none of this would have been possible, there would have been no high road to sustainable profitability for Panduit, if the company had not developed and patented its intellectual property.

It is absolutely essential to own what you sell. If Panduit had taken the one-piece cable tie to market without going to the trouble of filing a patent, there would have been nothing to stop competitors from copying their innovation. Through intellectual property rights, a company can establish an insurmountable commercial advantage over the competition. As was the case with the railroad barons of the 1870s, the first principal of modern technology entrepreneurs is to establish a monopoly. Technical monopolies are not as unqualified as railroad monopolies, but with competent management they can have the same effect in terms of profitability.

In addition to establishing a commercial advantage for a company's manufactured products, intellectual property by itself is also a product. Many companies derive substantial revenue by licensing their intellectual property to competitors. In 2001, for example, out of $87 million in earnings reported by the semiconductor company International Rectifier, $51 million came from net patent royalties. All the major semiconductor companies are engaged in licensing and cross-licensing technology and these activities have a net impact that adds to or subtracts from the bottom line.

The fact that semiconductor companies must in-license intellectual property to support their manufacturing activities has led to the emergence of a new kind of semiconductor company: one that doesn't manufacture anything. Instead, Rambus and similar companies skip the manufacturing part altogether and go directly from patenting technology to generating profits. It's the type of business model that appealed to investors in the eighties and nineties. By early 2000, Rambus stock was selling in the $170 range and seemed to be headed still higher. An analyst at UBS Warburg recommended it as a "strong buy" with a price target of

$350 per share. But it didn't happen. In June 2001, the stock was trading at $3, but has since recovered to about $18 in June 2003.

Rambus, by the way, is a profitable company that has been in business for more than twenty years. The company licenses its performance-enhancing technology to many of the world's largest semiconductor companies and, in spite of the precipitous fall in its stock price, the company appears to be sound. Whatever criticisms may be made of its business model, Rambus has done one thing well. If not, it would be unable to license its patents to some of the largest companies in the world. It has done an excellent job protecting its intellectual property.

Companies that do not protect their intellectual property have a different story to tell. In the mid-70s, Dan Bricklin did not patent the algorithms and interfaces he invented while a student at Harvard Business School and his partner, Bob Frankston, did not copyright the source code or graphical format of the software he wrote. Their product, VisiCalc, was the original spreadsheet program. Without patents the inventors could not prevent competition from copying their algorithms, and without copyrights the inventors could not prevent competition from copying their spreadsheet format. Their company, Personal Software Inc., did register a trademark for the new software product they had invented, but the registration for VisiCalc was cancelled in 1988 after the product had disappeared from the market and the brand name, presumably, had no further value. With the proper intellectual property protection, Bricklin and Frankston might have become major players in the software industry. Instead, they have the dubious distinction of founding, but not profiting from, a billion-dollar industry segment that grew to include SuperCalc®, Lotus®, Excel[ãã] and others.

There are three kinds of intellectual property protection that are important to technology companies—copyrights, trademarks and patents. Each type of protection has different rules and regulations and, depending on the details of your products and markets, may or may not be suitable for your company. A copyright prevents competitors from "reverse engineering" a product by making an exact copy. Companies in the music, publishing and broadcast industries are known for their use of copyrights. Less well known is the importance of this type of intellectual property to the technology industry. Semiconductor companies, for example, routinely protect the physical layout of their products by copyright. The international symbol for copyrighted material "©" followed by the name of the manufacturer and date is microscopically etched into the silicon substrate of many integrated circuits.

Software companies use copyrights to protect the source code of their programs and the layout or design of certain program features such as Graphical User Interfaces. While a copyright does not protect the underlying idea (but that might be protected by patent if it can be reduced to an algorithm), it does protect the form of expression. For example, if you were to develop a new computer language that subsequently became a standard of the industry, under copyright protection you could prevent competitors from using your syntax. A good example of opportunity lost in this respect is a programming language that was co-developed in 1964 by two professors at Dartmouth College, but Thomas Kurtz and John Kemeny never copyrighted their new language and it became public domain. Today, many of the big names in software sell versions of the most popular programming language in the world, BASIC. The inventors of the language receive occasional acknowledgement for their achievement, but no royalties.

Software companies can assert ownership of a copyright by including words such as, "Copyright 2002, Advanced Software Corporation," on the physical master (which should be archived in a secure location) and on all commercial copies of the product. Copyrights may be registered at the Copyright Office of the Library of Congress. For individual authors, the term of a copyright is life plus fifty years. If a corporation creates the material, copyrights are effective for seventy-five years.

Trademarks protect the commercial identity of a product. Consumer products companies regularly use trademarks to protect retail brand names. You can claim a trademark by simply placing the superscript "TM" after the word or phrase you wish to protect.

A registered trademark is one that has been registered at the United States Patent Office and is designated by the symbol "®" after the word or phrase that has been registered. Unlike other forms of intellectual property, trademarks can last forever and can be lost forever. "Aspirin," "corn flakes" and "cellophane" were once valid trademarks now forever lost due to improper use. Trademarks are obviously important to companies that sell to the retail consumer, but even some purely industrial companies place a high value on their trademarks and assiduously protect them.

Marlan Bourns, the inventor of the lead-screw actuated potentiometer and founder of the company that bears his name, was obsessed with the subject. In my capacity as a sales representative, during the 1970s I attended many Bourns sales conferences in Riverside, California. Sales conferences are primarily motivational affairs, but the Bourn's variety always included a stern lecture from the legal department on the proper use of registered trademarks. Of particular concern was the name "Trimpot©" that was so well known it was deemed to be in imminent danger of falling into the public domain. I can't say if Bourn's rigorous defense of its trademarks have been a key factor, but the company continues to be successful while many of its competitors are long since gone.

Another example of branding above and beyond the call of duty is Texas Instruments. When Varah Electronics was first appointed an authorized distributor of their semiconductors, we ordered an ad to publicize this fact in a national trade publication. The appointment was a big deal. The publisher, out of an abundance of caution, sent a pre-print of the ad to Texas Instruments. Immediately, a threatening call from Dallas instructed the ad to be pulled. We had gotten the logo—the stylized letters "T" and "I" within the outline of the great state of Texas—exactly right, but the color was wrong. It seems Texas Instruments "owned" a particular hue of the color brown and had a corporate mandate regarding its use. I'm sure members of the public would be astonished to learn that a color can be the property of a corporation.

However important copyrights and trademarks may be, the form of intellectual property that has generated more riches than any other is the patent. A patent is granted in the name of one or more persons but may be owned by a company, for example the inventor's employer, in which case the company is called the assignee. A patent conveys a 20-year monopoly. During this time period, products infringing the patent may be neither manufactured nor sold in the country where the patent issued. Generally speaking, an invention can be patented if it meets three tests: it must be novel, it must have utility, and it must be non-obvious to people skilled in the field of the invention. A patented invention is usually but not necessarily a physical thing. It is true that the three types of things that can never be patented—laws of nature, natural phenomena, and abstract ideas—are not physical things, but certain types of ideas such as algorithms can be patented. Having provided this gross oversimplification, a word of caution. Patents are complicated and interpretation should be left to the patent lawyers, who alone are able to comprehend the intricacies of the subject.

Patents protect either some physical thing, for example a control circuit for an electric motor, or a method that is used to manufacture physical things, for example a deposition process used in making high voltage transistors for many applications including a control circuit for an electric motor. As a general rule, method patents have a wider scope and are more valuable than patents that protect a specific physical product. In the biotechnology and pharmaceutical industries, however, just the opposite is true. In these industries, the most valuable intellectual property is called a composition of matter patent that protects the physical composition of a drug. For example, it is a composition of matter patent that enforces Pfizer's monopoly over the blockbuster drug Viagra®. Method patents in the biotechnology and pharmaceutical industries are not usually of great value, but there are exceptions. The polymerase chain reaction, a chemical procedure used to make millions of exact copies of a DNA sequence, not only resulted in a Nobel Prize for its inventor Kary Mullis, but also in the payment of three hundred million dollars to his employer, Cetus Corporation, when the patent was sold to the Swiss pharmaceutical company Roche.

Three hundred million dollars is a lot of money, but it pales in comparison to the amount of wealth generated by a single act of intellectual property outsourcing that occurred in 1980. That was the year IBM required an operating system for its new Personal Computer product line and selected Microsoft as the vendor. Microsoft, not possessing an operating system of their own, bought a license for 86-QDOS from Seattle Products for $25,000. 86-QDOS was reworked into the MS-DOS operating system that Microsoft licensed to IBM. The following year, Microsoft bought 86-QDOS outright for an additional payment of $50,000. During the process of becoming the world's most valuable company, Microsoft sold millions of copies of MS-DOS to IBM and hundreds of other companies that manufactured clones of the IBM Personal Computer.

There is another aspect to this episode in the early history of Microsoft. It is a story that comes, like the products of the company, in many different versions. This much of the story is true. Bill Gate's mother, Mary Gates, was a community leader active in charitable causes. Through her board-level participation in The United Way, she became friends with John Opel, the Chief Executive Officer of IBM. It was through this relationship that son Bill, a relatively inexperienced 24-year old, was able to gain access to the decision makers at IBM and close the business deal that started Microsoft on its way. Bill Gate's detractors have embellished these facts into a rather unpleasant yarn, but to my way of thinking the story highlights a basic principal of entrepreneurship: make the best possible use of your contacts.

In the industry of technology, two of the largest and most profitable segments consist of semiconductor companies and software companies. Microsoft, the largest and most profitable of the software companies, sells operating systems and got its start by outsourcing an operating system. Intel, the largest and most profitable of the chip companies, sells microcomputers and got its start by outsourcing a microcomputer. What's more, it paid good money for something it developed itself.

In 1971, the first Intel microcomputer was originally designed as a custom product for the Japanese company Busicom. Intel's customer had ordered a calculator chip set but what they got was something very different. Ted Hoff, the designer of the 4004, built a general-purpose logic device that retrieved its instructions from semiconductor memory in contrast to a traditional "hard wired" calculator chip set. According to the version of the story that circulated at the time, Busicom were not very happy with what they had received. An unhappy customer rises to the attention of the people in charge, and soon the senior management of Intel was embroiled in debate. The company's founders, Robert Noyce and Gordon Moore, thought the new approach to designing logic circuits had great promise and became advocates for the idea. But a large part of the management team thought the microcomputer would be a distraction to Intel's principal business. Intel was founded in 1968 to address a considerable challenge: make semiconductor memory practical. Three years later, here was Intel flirting with a new direction. Where was the focus? Any self-respecting consultant would have advised Intel to concentrate on their core product of semiconductor memory. But Noyce and Moore had their way, in retrospect it's called leadership, and Intel bought back the rights to the 4004 from Busicom for $60,000. The rest is history.

Today, many technology companies outsource at least some of their intellectual property and the biggest vendors in this marketplace are the universities. It appears almost every educational institution in the land has gotten into the act. A search of Google in June 2003 for the combination "intellectual property" and "license" and "university" returned more than 200,000 hits. Shopping the universities for intellectual property is an especially common practice for startup technology companies. In the best deals, the fledgling company receives not only the intellectual property but also the university professor who developed the technology as a scientific adviser. Deals with an attached professor may be more complex than a straightforward license, but they can sometimes be easier to consummate because the professor becomes an internal champion for the deal. In addition, having the professor on board usually reduces the implementation risk of a new technology.

The point of this section is simple: all modern businesses, however large or small, need intellectual property. A small service business, a restaurant or a company that resurfaces driveways, needs to protect its name or else the intangible value that every business accumulates over time will be next to worthless. For the same reason, any manufacturing company needs at minimum to own the names of its products. For a technology company, where the product *is* the technology, intellectual property is even more important. Not only does it allow the accumulation of intangible value for the future, but also enables higher margins in the present. For these reasons, before starting a technology company you must understand exactly what intellectual property you will need and how you will get it. This understanding needs to come at the beginning, even before your new company is incorporated. Until you have it, don't quit your day job.

CHAPTER THREE

Startup

"The person who says it cannot be done should not interrupt the person who is doing it."
Chinese proverb

Starting a business has never been easy, but the uncertainties of recent times have made it significantly more difficult especially when it comes to financing the startup. A few years ago, there were bank loan guarantees and direct funding available from local, state, and federal government programs. Today, the priorities of governments have changed, funding for new business has almost completely dried up, and the banks won't talk to you. A few years ago, venture capital investors were searching for growth and new opportunities. Today, cash is king. The venture capitalists have moved from financing the future to financing the present. They are looking for profits not growth, performance not opportunity. Today, the entrepreneur has no choice except to finance the startup with his or her own money, and then adopt a rather conservative approach in building the business.

A conservative approach may run counter to the natural instincts of someone courageous enough to start his or her own business, but there is no reasonable alternative. Without outside institutions or investors to share the risk, when the money runs out, you are not only out of business but very likely facing personal bankruptcy. With your livelihood and ego on the line, the path advocated is to carefully plan, diligently execute, and always leave something in reserve to provide for the unforeseen.

Starting a business does not begin with the process of

incorporation. It is important to suppress that first instinct to visit the lawyer in the local strip mall or, even worse, respond to the classified ad promising to incorporate your company for one hundred dollars. Instead, the process begins with recruiting the professionals, at minimum a corporate lawyer and an accountant, who will ensure you do things right from the beginning. However, bear the following proviso in mind: one-third of all lawyers and accountants graduated in the lowest third of their class. Look for bandwidth and content, intelligence and experience. Buy as much horsepower as you can get.

Hire your lawyer first. Ask your business friends about their lawyers, and listen carefully to what each friend says. You need a lawyer with experience in corporate law who will be able to understand not just your instructions but also your intent. You need someone who will accept your leadership and direction but will be a forceful advocate in terms of what is legal and what is practical. This person will become your friend, and your job is to find someone with whom, over time, you can build such a relationship. Don't ask your business friend if his or her lawyer is competent, ask about the lawyer's practice. Does the firm specialize in business law, real estate transactions, personal injury cases, or divorces? If there is no obvious business focus, thank you friend and move on. If the firm does have a business focus, ask you friend to tell you something about the lawyer's personal life and interests. If you like what you hear, it's time to make a phone call.

Most lawyers, even the busiest, will meet with a prospective new client who has been referred by an existing client. Tell the lawyer you plan to incorporate a new business and want the right lawyer from the start. Every lawyer will agree with the logic of your premise. From the point of view of a corporate lawyer, in the beginning their clients' legal affairs are usually in a shambles and their first job is to clean up past mistakes. Mention you have no problem with an associate doing the work, but you want experienced oversight to ensure everything is done correctly. Explain how you plan to change the world, fill in a few details about your personal life, and listen. Are you having a conversation? Do you like what you hear? If so, you may have found your lawyer.

If the intellectual property protection you seek is not complicated, for example registering a trademark to protect the name of the business, a good corporate lawyer is all the legal talent you will need. If, however, the intellectual property requirements are more complicated, for example filing a patent, you will need a separate lawyer to deal with these issues. What you seek is a person who is three things in one: a lawyer, a patent agent, and someone with experience in your technical field. These rare individuals are usually overloaded with work and are not looking for new clients. However, your corporate lawyer can help you get your foot in the door. Every good corporate lawyer loves the law and knows other lawyers who love the law. Through the one, you will find the other. Again, your intellectual property lawyer will parcel out the grunt work to associates. But this is fine. The trouble with any intellectual property, for example a patent, is its value is difficult to establish until some future date when a competitor challenges its validity in court. Your expert will review the associates' work to ensure a quality product that will stand the test of time.

In the first meeting with your intellectual property lawyer, set up a timetable and stick to it. Chances are the lawyer will want to file a disclosure as soon as possible with the United States Patent Office to establish the earliest possible effective date. The next step is to file a patent application in the United States, after which you have twelve months to make a PCT (Patent Cooperation Treaty) filing that protects your right to file in other countries. With patents, timing is the most important thing. If you don't carefully budget what time is available, the costs of protecting your intellectual property can dramatically increase. As an experienced intellectual property lawyer named Brian Gray puts it, "I have three deliverables—speed, accuracy and low cost—and you can have any two of them."

Having secured top legal talent, your next task is to hire an accountant. Again, to find the right accountant you will need a personal reference and, again, the best place to obtain it is from your corporate lawyer. Look for an open mind. Most accountants think all things fit into defined categories. They are fundamentalists, unequipped to deal with nuance, who believe in Generally Accepted Accounting Principles as fervently as Mississippi Baptists believe in the Ten Commandments. Once again, less knowledgeable associates may actually be responsible for much of the work, but your experienced accountant will make sure things are done right. It is less important to have a personal relationship with your accountant, but it helps.

Having recruited the professional talent you will need in the future, it's back to the present. It's time to incorporate. However intimidating the process may sound, incorporating a company is routine work for a competent lawyer. For tax reasons, your lawyer may recommend setting up your company as a Delaware corporation. This is a practical option because you don't have to incorporate in the state where you will carry on business. I have been a director of several companies incorporated in Delaware, but not one of these companies was located in Delaware. By themselves, tax considerations are usually the wrong reasons to decide important issues, but Delaware is also known for its streamlined paperwork system and that, at least, is a reasonable basis for a business decision. My advice is to go with the incorporating jurisdiction recommended by your lawyer. It's one less decision to make.

Your lawyer will require a prioritized list of names for your company that can be checked against a database of names to determine availability. For the purposes of this book, "New Products Corporation" is the name I have used. I hope you can come up with a better name than that. Another item you can prepare in advance is a paragraph that describes the business of the company. This particular bit of information is not always required, but you will be surprised how difficult it can be to compose one concise paragraph, so have it prepared in advance. It is helpful to set this short description to memory. Everybody you come into contact with in your personal life, if you have a personal life, will want to know about your company in one paragraph's worth of detail.

Your also need to determine the number of shares the company will issue and its initial capitalization. The initial capitalization, since you have no partners, is the amount of money you will pay for your shares. Whatever you decide to pay for your shares, I suggest you have two million shares issued in return because this number of shares provides the greatest possible flexibility in the future. If the company remains a closely held private corporation that finances its growth through retained earnings, the number of shares is unimportant. However, if it is decided at a future date to raise external capital, starting out with two million shares will reduce the likelihood that the company will have to reorganize its capital structure with a share split or reverse split. In a share split, the outstanding number of shares is increased, for example every "old" share is converted into two "new" shares in a 2:1 split. In a reverse split, the outstanding number of shares is decreased, for example every two "old" shares are converted into one "new" share in a 1:2 reverse split. A mountain of paperwork can be avoided by issuing the right number of shares at the beginning.

The initial capitalization is the amount of money you intend to put into the company and *leave* in the company. In a typical example, the entrepreneur might pay $20,000 in return for 2,000,000 Common Shares at a price of $0.01 each, and the initial capitalization of the company would in this case be $20,000. Sometimes, for example to establish a good relationship with the bank and suppliers, you might want the company to start out with more than the initial capitalization in its bank account. If so, you can loan funds to the company in addition to the $20,000 you invested in your shares. The additional funds must, of course, be treated as a loan, but as chief executive you can have the company repay all or part of the loan at any time. On the other hand, the company cannot return any of the $20,000 you have paid for your shares without the prior written permission of the shareholders and a significant amount of legal paperwork.

The new company will require a Board of Directors. Contrary to what seems to be usual practice based on how often it is done, membership on the Board of Directors is not an appropriate honor to bestow upon your friends. Instead, you need experienced people familiar with your business and willing to contribute to its success. Unless you have already identified such people and they have agreed to serve on the Board, instruct your lawyer to prepare the paperwork for a Board of Directors of five persons, with two of the five positions vacant. The vacant positions can be filled at any time by a resolution of the Board. The starting Board of three members will be composed of you and two individuals who understand their appointments are temporary until permanent Board members can be recruited. The best candidates for these interim positions may be your spouse and your lawyer.

At this point, with the underlying intellectual property well understood and the company properly incorporated, there are two directions that may be taken and the appropriate course depends on the financial position of the entrepreneur. Very occasionally, new entrepreneurs have enough personal wealth to finance the company until it becomes self-sufficient in terms of cash flow. More often, the entrepreneur is long on ideas and energy, but short on cash. This is the direction my narrative will follow. If you are lucky enough to fall into the high net worth financial category, please accept my apologies and my congratulations.

In the beginning, your priority is probably not to build a profitable company. Chances are you do not have enough money to finance the building of a profitable company; therefore, your priority can only be to build the company to the point your existing personal finances allow. At that point, you need to convince your friends and relatives your project has merit. Your friends and relatives will want to understand the opportunity before they invest but, however well your friends and relatives may think they understand what they are getting into, their primary motivation to invest is a personal belief in your judgement and abilities. It is a matter of trust and it is serious. Therefore, before asking your friends and relatives for money, you need to be absolutely confident that the potential benefits justify the risks. In the example of New Products Corporation, the entrepreneur has six months to achieve this elevated level of confidence.

The first six months are the most critical period in the life of a new technology company because many diverse projects need to be completed within a limited amount of time and under the constraint of a relatively inflexible budget. To be successful, it is imperative to know what you intend to do, when you will do it, and how you will pay for it. The plan covering the first six months is for your personal use and can be rather informal, but it must be complete.

During the first six months, there are two goals the company must achieve. It must establish an intellectual property position, and it must demonstrate that its proposed product incorporating the intellectual property is technically feasible and commercially viable. Drafting and filing high-quality patent applications can be mentally demanding, but the work itself is relatively straightforward. Building a prototype or otherwise establishing technical feasibility can also be routine work, but establishing commercial viability can be difficult.

There is only one sure-fire way to establish the commercial viability of a new product, and that is by talking to customers. It is absolutely essential for an entrepreneur, however deeply he or she may believe in the initial design of the prototype, to obtain the unbiased opinions of customers before the product's commercial launch. The assumptions made during the design stage need to be validated. For example, the intended product must not only be priced competitively, but also be compatible with the physical and performance requirements of your customers. In addition to confirming the proper design of a product, there are practical business reasons to solicit the opinions of customers at an early stage. There is a certain courtship between sellers and buyers in which a period of time, usually a longer period than the vendor would prefer, precedes the buying decision. This is the time lag Adam Osborne sought to overcome by pre-announcing his computer systems. While, as we have seen, the strategy of pre-announcement can be perilous for an established company, it works beautifully for a new company. The sooner you establish relationships with customers, the sooner you will begin to sell products.

Nevertheless, in a rush to bring a new product to market, entrepreneurs often put off the inconvenience of visiting customers until the product has been fully developed. Such procrastination can lead to disastrous consequences, and it is a lesson I learned the hard way. Some years ago, I founded Annulus Technical Industries, a manufacturing company in the high-density electrical switch business. During the first year, I filed the patent (U.S. 4,680,433, if you are interested), rented a few thousand square feet in an industrial complex, designed and built a prototype, tested it and found it satisfactory, rushed it into production, prepared marketing materials and sent new product announcements to trade magazines. All was going well. Even my sales strategy, to let the customers come to me, seemed to be working. The orders started rolling in. It was only then that I discovered the design was incompatible with the wave soldering process used by more than 90% of the potential customers. The product had to be completely redesigned. The financial loss was considerable, but even more significant was the loss of a full year.

In addition to establishing an intellectual property position, and demonstrating through customer consultations that the proposed product is technically feasible and commercially viable, there are a number of other activities that must be completed during the first six months. Unless it is practical for the entrepreneur to work from home, a suitable location needs to be rented and equipped with a telephone, computer, fax machine, printer, copier, and office supplies. Legal documents including a Confidential Disclosure Agreement and Shareholders' Agreement need to be prepared. The Business Plan including the Seed Round Financial Forecast must be written and, finally, the seed round financing must be completed.

At New Products Company, the company budgets $6,000 for six months rent of a temporary office that includes telephone service and access to business equipment, $5,000 for legal and patent costs, $5,000 for developing a prototype, and $6,000 for other expenses. This totals $22,000 during six months, but the company only has $20,000 in its bank account from your purchase of shares.

You should be prepared to make up the shortfall, and also to meet your personal living expenses for six months. Some of this cash may come from a bank in the form of loans, but these will be personal loans. No bank I know of will lend pre-seed money to a startup business. If you do plan to borrow from the bank, keep in mind that personal bankers expect borrowers to have a regular income from an arms-length employer. Under this definition, you may no longer qualify as gainfully employed, and will therefore no longer qualify for most personal loans. It is dangerous to use an unsecured personal credit line to finance a startup because it may be revoked when the bank learns you have become self-employed, but a home equity loan is fine. A home equity loan will not be revoked as long as you make the payments.

The best sources for startup capital are personal savings, home equity loans and the holy trinity: Visa, MasterCard and American Express. More than one startup has been launched with credit card debt. Your automobile can be sold for cash and a replacement leased. You can borrow from friends or family. You can sell your sailboat, coin collection and other non-essential assets. But whatever the source of your pre-seed money, make sure all of it is in place before striking out on your own.

During these first six months, you will receive no salary. There are three good reasons why the company will not be in a position to compensate you for your efforts. First of all, the company cannot afford to pay salaries because there are no salaries in the budget. Secondly, if the company were to pay a salary to the individual who has provided the company with its sole source of funds, it would be a foolish use of cash. When you pay yourself with your own money, the only beneficiary is the taxman. Thirdly, and most importantly, the unpaid time you spend on behalf of the company is the "sweat equity" that entitles you to own a large number of extremely inexpensive shares compared to the price the seed investors will be required to pay.

CHAPTER FOUR

The Seed Round

"Money is the seed of money."
Jean Jacques Rousseau

Because the universe of potential investors in your new company is severely restricted by law, the seed round begins with a visit to your lawyer. The purpose of securities law is to protect the investing public. To this end, a substantial body of state and federal legislation exists to regulate how companies raise capital. While I provide some guidance about securities law and related subjects, my intent is merely educational. The more you know about a subject, even if some of that knowledge is imperfect, the better equipped you will be to ask meaningful questions of your legal advisors and to understand the advice received. However, in all cases and under any conditions whatsoever, you must rely solely on the advice of your lawyer for guidance in all matters pertaining to securities law. Now, that's a disclaimer.

In my opinion, the best guideline for passage through this legal minefield law is to always keep in mind the concept of "eligible investor." It is, after all, in our dealings with investors that we receive the highest level of regulatory scrutiny and are subject to the most severe penalties if our conduct is found wanting. An eligible investor, simply put, is some party—person or institution—that can legally buy stock in your company. Depending on the specific details of the financing activity, there will be a provision in securities law defining eligibility. If you combine the knowledge of which investors are eligible investors with a little common sense, you will arrive at three guidelines to avoid legal problems when your company raises capital. First, follow the advice of your lawyer. Second, truthfully disclose all material facts. Third, never allow shares in your company to be sold to any party that is not an eligible investor. You must rely on the advice of your lawyer to determine the legal process for raising seed capital in your jurisdiction. There may be certain procedures you will have to follow, such as establishing the relationship between you and prospective investors, or a limit to the number of people who may receive a solicitation, or a requirement to record the distribution of materials, or a limit on the amount to be raised, or a limit on the number of shareholders. As a general rule, however, there will be provisions in the law that allow you to raise seed capital for your startup company by selling shares to a legally restricted group of people. Members of this group, usually but not always including family, friends, and close business associates, are eligible investors.

Having a general idea of who would qualify as an eligible investor in your jurisdiction, make a list of prospective investors and discuss it with your lawyer. If you are having difficulty assembling such a list, here are a few pointers. Your dentist, doctor, the person who prepares your income tax, your bank manager and similar people may have two important qualifications for inclusion on your list—they may know you well and they probably have money to invest. Previous bosses and co-workers know you well and might be interested in investing in your new venture. Consider others you came to know well in your working career: people who worked for the competition, former customers and suppliers, those you came to know at trade shows or seminars. Then of course there are the old standbys of relatives, and friends from college and high school. How much can you raise? Write an estimate next to each name and divide the total in half. That's your number. For our purposes, the entrepreneur has determined his friends and family will be prepared to invest $300,000 in New Products Corporation.

Of the two documents that should be prepared before approaching potential investors—a Business Plan and a Seed Round Financial Forecast—for me it is easier to start with the numbers. I find it far less complicated to think through the various issues, especially those that are interrelated, in numerical terms, so I begin with the Seed Round Financial Forecast. After I've massaged the entries in my spreadsheet program for a few hours, my tentative understanding of the new company matures into something that can be described in writing.

The Seed Round Financial Forecast contains enough financial information, and in sufficient detail, to allow the entrepreneur to make good business decisions, yet it is easy to understand by relatively unsophisticated investors. Each of the columns represents one month of the forecast period. The focus of this spreadsheet is the company's cash position, the starting value at the beginning and the ending value at the completion of each month. Cash is the most important factor to a startup technology company. Cash means survival. Unrestrained and without focus, technology companies can burn a great deal of cash and, when the cash is gone, the company fails. We expect our startup company to burn cash in the beginning, but our goal is to turn the corner on cash flow no later than twelve months after completion of the seed round.

If our goal, indeed our requirement for survival, is to generate cash, then of necessity our singular focus in running the enterprise must be sales. It is an uncomfortable but undeniable fact that the only way a company can generate cash is to sell something. It is for this reason that the process of building the Seed Round Financial Forecast must begin with a sales forecast. A sales forecast starting from zero that *must be achieved* is an intimidating exercise, and it is unavoidable. You are not only responsible for the forecast but also for making it happen, and the penalty for non-performance is personal catastrophe. Building a sales forecast is a litmus test for entrepreneurial talent. If you can't do it, maybe this is the wrong career choice. As Dirty Harry said in *Magnum Force*, "A man's got to know his limitations." But, assuming you are up to the task, once the sales forecast has been completed, every business decision your make must contribute to meeting the sales milestones.

Having stressed the importance of sales, it is necessary to address the issue of financial control. It is possible, in fact it happens quite frequently, for companies to meet their sales forecasts yet get into serious financial trouble or worse. In addition to sales, entrepreneurs must also manage the rest of the business, and in particular control cash. In Table 1, four important operational measurements that impact cash—inventory, accounts receivable, capital costs, and expenses—run down the left side of the Seed Round Financial Forecast.

Materials purchased, materials consumed, and ending inventory, are forecast for each month. It is assumed that the company must purchase component parts for its products and these items will begin to accumulate in inventory beginning with Month 1. By the end of the forecast period, the amount of materials purchased is approximately equal to the amount of materials consumed in each month. The spreadsheet automatically calculates the amount of materials consumed as 20% of sales for each month. The company plans to ship its manufacturing output directly to customers to keep finished goods inventory to a minimum. At the end of the forecast period, the total inventory is about equal to the materials needed to manufacture one month's sales. When finished goods are in inventory at the end of the month, this format reports only the value of the purchased components within the finished goods.

The following line, accounts receivable, is the amount of money owed to the company by its customers. The spreadsheet assumes that accounts receivable will equal total sales in the current plus the previous month. In accounting terms, the aging of the accounts receivable is 60 days because the total amount owed by customers equals the amount the company sells to customers in 60 days. Companies that efficiently collect outstanding invoices can do better than 60 days, but 60 days is a reasonable estimate for forecast purposes.

Capital costs include production and test equipment, furniture and office equipment, and leasehold improvements. You may have a specific list of capital expenditures your business will need to make. If not, start with an estimate of $4,000 for each employee with a desk and computer, and add the cost of facilities and

Month after seed round:					
	1	*2*	*3*	*4*	*5*
Starting cash	300,000	277,000	224,000	176,000	138,000
Sales	0	0	5,000	15,000	20,000
Materials purchased	3,000	3,000	3,000	3,000	4,000
Materials consumed	0	0	1,000	3,000	4,000
Inventory	3,000	6,000	8,000	8,000	8,000
Accounts Receivable	0	0	5,000	20,000	35,000
Capital costs	5,000	25,000	20,000	10,000	0
Expenses:					
Salaries and Benefits	5,000	15,000	15,000	15,000	17,000
Rent	3,000	3,000	3,000	3,000	3,000
Communications	1,000	1,000	1,000	1,000	1,000
Office	1,000	1,000	1,000	1,000	1,000
Travel	1,000	1,000	1,000	1,000	1,000
Professional fees	2,000	2,000	2,000	2,000	2,000
Utilities	1,000	1,000	1,000	1,000	1,000
Other	1,000	1,000	1,000	1,000	1,000
Cash generated (burned)	-23,000	-53,000	-48,000	-38,000	-26,000
Ending cash	277,000	224,000	176,000	138,000	112,000

Table 1. Seed Round

6	7	8	9	10	11	12
112,000	94,000	79,000	67,000	60,000	56,000	51,000
30,000	30,000	35,000	35,000	40,000	45,000	45,000
6,000	6,000	8,000	8,000	8,000	9,000	9,000
6,000	6,000	7,000	7,000	8,000	9,000	9,000
8,000	8,000	9,000	10,000	10,000	10,000	10,000
50,000	60,000	65,000	70,000	75,000	85,000	90,000
0	0	5,000	0	0	0	0
17,000	19,000	19,000	19,000	21,000	21,000	21,000
3,000	3,000	3,000	3,000	3,000	3,000	3,000
1,000	1,000	1,000	1,000	1,000	1,000	1,000
1,000	1,000	1,000	1,000	1,000	1,000	1,000
1,000	1,000	1,000	1,000	1,000	1,000	1,000
2,000	2,000	2,000	2,000	2,000	2,000	2,000
1,000	1,000	1,000	1,000	1,000	1,000	1,000
1,000	1,000	1,000	1,000	1,000	1,000	1,000
-18,000	-15,000	-12,000	-7,000	-4,000	-5,000	0
94,000	79,000	67,000	60,000	56,000	51,000	51,000

Financial Forecast

equipment needed to manufacture, test and package your product. Most of the capital costs will occur during the beginning months, but it is prudent to leave a cushion for the unexpected as in the example where $5,000 is listed under Month 8.

A convenient method to project expenses is to start with payroll. Make a list of people to be hired including salaries and timing. In the example, your personal salary (including benefits) is $60,000 per year. Your first hires occur in Month 2 with a senior manager at $48,000 per year, and a front office person and a production supervisor at $36,000 annually each. Therefore salaries and benefits in Month 1 total $5,000 but jump to $15,000 in Month 2. Three hourly production employees, at $2,000 each per month, are added during the forecast period. Once the number and composition of staff have been determined, the remaining expenses are easier to estimate. Rent, office, travel, utilities and other expenses can be estimated from the standpoint of facilities and head count. Travel and communications expense will be related to the geographic distribution of customers. In the example, the total expenses for professional fees including legal, patent, and accounting are estimated at $24,000 for the full year and are charged to the forecast on a straight-line basis at $2,000 per month.

The Seed Round Financial Forecast reflects a number of assumptions and some will prove to be erroneous. From time to time you will need to make changes. The essential factor is to put together a plan that supports the sales milestones, and achieves a near-positive cash flow with a cash cushion by the end of Month 12. The spreadsheet calculates the amount of cash generated or burned in a month using the following algorithm: sales minus materials consumed, minus the month's increase in accounts receivable (or plus a decrease), minus capital costs, minus expenses. During the period covered by the forecast, the biggest drain on cash is the financing of accounts receivable. At the end of the twelfth month, the company will be owed $90,000 by its customers.

Having completed a detailed numerical description of the business, the text of the Business Plan should fall into place. Write a few pages describing the company's technology, products and markets. Describe the company's sales milestones and how they will be achieved. Insert a copy of the Seed Round Financial Forecast with commentary, and explain why you believe it is achievable. Make clear that you expect changes will have to be made to the plan, but you believe the plan is sufficiently flexible to allow the company to achieve its objectives. For example, with $90,000 in accounts receivable at the end of Month 12 that can be used as collateral, if needed the company should be able to arrange a bank credit line of at least $45,000. Briefly explain your vision for the future of the company including how and when you expect the company will be in a position to pay dividends or provide some form of financial liquidity to its shareholders. Also be sure to include a section in the Business Plan that clearly outlines the risks. Your lawyer can provide guidance on this subject.

In addition to writing a paragraph or two for the Business Plan, instruct your lawyer to prepare a Confidential Disclosure Agreement and a Shareholders' Agreement. The first document is a standard agreement you will use many times in the future, for example whenever you need to disclose confidential information about manufacturing processes to a customer. Before you discuss any aspect of your business with a prospective seed investor, require them to sign a Confidential Disclosure Agreement. In addition to protecting the company's confidential information, there is nothing better to set the right tone, namely, this is a valuable opportunity that needs to be protected.

A Shareholders' Agreement is a document that defines the terms and conditions of being a shareholder in your company. You are particularly interested in simplifying the approval process for future financings should they become desirable or necessary. Ideally, you want to be able to negotiate and close future financings on whatever terms are deemed appropriate at the time by the Board of Directors. The important point to remember is this: if you wish to restrict the rights of certain shareholders, in this case seed round investors, you have to do it up front. Once an investment has been made, it is usually difficult to change the terms. Before the fact, however, it is perfectly acceptable to explain that the purchase of shares will require signing the Shareholders' Agreement that places certain limitations on the rights of shareholders.

While on the subject of legalities, a few comments about lawyers are in order. Your lawyer is not there to tell you what to do. Your lawyer's job is to recommend the best legal strategy to accomplish your objectives. Decide what you want to do before walking into the lawyer's office. If you start by knowing what you want, you will save your lawyer's time and your company's money. Your lawyer will charge a reasonable fee for his or her time and you should be prepared to pay it, because real value accrues through conducting your affairs in a legal manner. It's also important, in my opinion, to conduct your affairs in an ethical manner, but don't ask your lawyer for advice on this subject. Advice as to what is or is not ethical is available from numerous sources, and usually free of charge.

In a seed round financing of under $1 million, the amount of equity sold ranges between 10% and 30%. I have selected a number in the middle of this range, 20%, for New Products Corporation. If this seems arbitrary, the calculation to determine the number and price of the shares to be sold will seem even more so, because the calculation depends on the amount to be raised instead of a valuation of the company itself. Of course the company does have value. There is value in the intellectual property owned by the company, there is value in the transformation of intellectual property into a business model, and there is the value that accrued during the first six months of the company's operations. But it is very difficult, if not impossible, to derive an objective valuation based on these criteria.

Since a fixed percentage of the company is to be sold, the amount of capital raised determines valuation. For example, if you raise $500,000 in return for 20% of your company, the pre-money valuation is $2,000,000 and the post-money valuation is $2,500,000. But if you were to raise $250,000 in seed capital, the pre-money valuation would be $1,000,000 and the post-money valuation $1,250,000. The large difference in valuation is justifiable because the value of a technology company depends more on what it will do in the future than on what has been accomplished in the past. A company with $500,000 in working capital will necessarily be worth more than the identical company with only $250,000. In our example, New Products Corporation receives $300,000 in seed capital in return for 20% of the post-money ownership, therefore the pre-money valuation is $1,200,000 and the post-money valuation is $1,500,000. A total of 2,000,000 Common Shares have been issued prior to the seed round, therefore New Products Corporation must issue 500,000 Common Shares at a price of sixty cents per share for the math to come out right.

After receiving guidance from your lawyer about eligible investors and the other legalities of the process, it is time to talk with the people on your list. Be straightforward about the reason for your visit. Explain to each prospect that you have started a new company and are putting together a group of seed round investors. Take no more than five minutes to explain what your company hopes to achieve in terms of product and sales milestones. It is important to stress, however enthusiastic you may be, that the venture is speculative and not appropriate for people who cannot afford to lose their investment. If there is interest, and after the prospective investor signs the Confidential Disclosure Agreement, leave a copy of your prepared materials. Promise to follow up in three days. Give the prospective investor sufficient time to consider your proposal, but within a limited window of opportunity.

Begin your follow up call with a short review of the company and the terms of the proposed investment. Then remind the prospective investor that the amount of money most people spend in a month is not much less than the amount they earn, and it is becoming increasingly difficult to accumulate significant personal wealth through savings and traditional investments. A successful investment in an early stage company, however, can generate a substantial return. On the other hand, these investments are risky. Don't gloss over the subject of risk. No investor seeks out increased risk, but an investment promising a big return with little risk is a red flag. It is always better to overstate rather than understate risk, but put it into perspective. If you believe the potential return is higher than the probable risk, say so and explain your reasons. Finally, ask for a non-binding expression of interest for a specific dollar amount.

Inevitably, one or more of your prospects will expect a seat on the company's Board of Directors in return for their financial support. This demand, an understandable if somewhat naive expectation, is a potential deal-breaker requiring a carefully worded response. If the prospect is a large investor, you may wish to offer a Board seat in return for a firm commitment. If the prospect is not a large investor and you want to provide encouragement only, explain the seed round investors will elect one or two board members for a twelve-month term.

From the first contact with a prospective investor until you close the financing, most of your time should be dedicated to the project. Your aim is to close the financing four weeks after receiving the first non-binding expression of interest. Follow up as many times and with as much additional information as is needed to satisfy each potential investor. Keep a "book" of the running total of firm commitments. If your book is not full after two weeks, kick your system into overdrive. If, at the end of three weeks, the book is still not full, you may have to settle for the lower number. In this case, rework the Seed Round Financial Forecast and Business Plan and explain the changes to the committed investors prior to closing. When the book is full, phone the prospective investors with the good news: the financing will close in one week. Give them a specific date. Arrange to deliver copies of the closing documents for their review and the review of their legal counsel. Make an appointment with each investor, for a date and time prior to the closing, to pick up his or her check and the signed documentation.

After the seed round has been closed and the proceeds deposited into the company's bank account, take a week off to recharge your batteries and get reconnected to the people you care about. In the back of your mind you will continue to think about the task ahead, but your only business-related activities will be to purchase four times as many tee shirts as you have seed round investors and to arrange the closing dinner. Hire a meeting room in a nice, but not expensive, hotel, and order a catered dinner of rubber chicken with a cash bar. Have the name of the company printed on the tee shirts. Closing dinners are important rites of passage, especially for the spouses. There should be a podium and a sign, or a banner, with the name of the company. You need to personally greet each guest and, at some point during your remarks, which should be brief and delivered after dinner, mention each investor by name.

CHAPTER FIVE

A Product-Oriented Strategy

"You cannot always control what goes on outside.
But you can always control what goes on inside."
Wayne Dyer

In the summer of 1958, Jack Kilby of Texas Instruments fabricated the first integrated circuit, a phase-shift oscillator, on a tiny bar-shaped piece of germanium. Incidentally, to this day engineers at Texas Instruments refer to unpackaged semiconductors as "bars" while to the rest of the world they are known as "dice." Six months after Kilby's achievement, Robert Noyce, working at the startup Fairchild Semiconductor of which he was a founder, also built a working integrated circuit. But his device had several advantages. The Noyce circuit was fabricated on silicon, a better material for integrated circuits, and it employed the planar process that was eventually used for the inexpensive mass production of the new devices. In 1961, the first commercial grade integrated circuits were introduced by Fairchild Semiconductor and Texas Instruments. Robert Noyce died at the relatively young age of 62 in 1990; otherwise he would certainly have shared in the 2000 Nobel Prize in Physics awarded to Jack Kilby.

Tom Wolfe tells a wonderful story in his essay *Robert Noyce and His Congregation*, published in the Forbes magazine supplement *ASAP* in 1997. A young engineer was put in charge of a major project, something Noyce advocated first at Fairchild Semiconductor and later at Intel Corporation, and came upon a difficult problem. He went to Noyce, explained the issue, and asked for guidance:

> And Noyce would lower his head, turn on his 100-ampere eyes, listen, and say: "Look, here are your guidelines. You've got to consider A, you've got to consider B, and you've got to consider C." Then he would turn on the Gary Cooper smile: "But if you think I'm going to make your decision for you, you're mistaken. Hey . . . it's your ass."

In my opinion, even though few business strategy consultants would agree, in early stage technology companies the entrepreneur's leadership ability is the most important factor to the eventual success or failure of the enterprise. While performance in larger organizations can be induced through management directives, in smaller companies employees need to be motivated to consistently perform at high levels. Robert Noyce not only had an intimate knowledge of the needs and aspirations of technical people, but was also a natural leader whose leadership skills compensated for Intel's lack of strategic direction during its formative years.

Intel was founded with the expressed purpose of making semiconductor memories practical. It was a product-oriented strategy. However, within a few years the company's direction changed from the memory business to the microcomputer business. The strategy changed, but history has shown that changing the direction of Intel was the right decision. Having found an even better product-oriented strategy, one with a multi-billion dollar potential, one would think Intel would focus all of its energies on its new single-minded pursuit. But that didn't happen. In the coming years, Intel made major forays into a number of completely different products outside its area of expertise. The company introduced the 2920, one of the earliest digital signal processors, and the im7110, a magnetic bubble memory device, and the iSBC product line of industrial computer board-level products. At one point, Intel even made an incursion into the digital watch business with their Microma division that introduced the first timepiece with a liquid crystal display.

While it is dangerous to argue with success, the formative years of Intel are not a very good role model for an entrepreneur developing a product-oriented strategy. However, we can learn an important lesson from Intel's experience: it is better to make good product decisions before the market does it for you. Intel lost its original focus on semiconductor memories and the market eventually forced the company out of the commodity memory business while competitors with a focus in the area, for example Micron Technology, continue to thrive. Later, Intel saw an opportunity in digital signal processors so it got into that business, too, but the market eventually forced Intel out while competitors with more focus, for example Texas Instruments, continue to thrive. Intel also became for a time the largest supplier of magnetic bubble memories. However, the adventure was short-lived when semiconductor memories, Intel's one-time mission in life, made magnetic bubble memories obsolete. Intel saw an opportunity in the industrial board-level product business and made a major investment in the area that lasted for many years. Eventually, however, competitors with more focus selling the alternative VME board-level format took over the market. As for Microma watches, to this day I have no idea why Intel got into that business. But there remains a certain personal consolation. I was given a Microma watch as a sales inducement and one day I hope to take it to the *Antiques Roadshow*.

Whether it comes as the result of executing a Business Plan or, less efficiently and with greater pain, through market forces, most successful technology companies eventually wind up with a product-oriented strategy. Implementing a product-oriented strategy is no easy matter, but there is no sensible alternative. The best policy is to limit the company's product line to items that address the needs of a single customer base and can be efficiently taken to market through the same channel. For example, a company that makes transistors for the communications industry and has built a customer base in that industry will have a poor channel for transistors used by the computer industry. But even more significantly, a company that makes transistors and has trained a sales organization to sell transistors will have no effective channel at all for new products that are not transistors. In addition to channel, a product-oriented strategy must take manufacturability and saleability into consideration. There is little sense in building a sales channel for products that cannot be manufactured in the required quantities, or within the required time frame, or at the required cost.

For example, consider the fate of Litronix, one of the first companies in the light emitting diode business. Today, these inexpensive semiconductor devices have almost completely supplanted the use of miniature incandescent and neon bulbs. But in the beginning, light emitting diodes were the new kid on the block, relatively expensive, and fighting for market share. Litronix management correctly assumed that the market would eventually be huge, but incorrectly assumed that there would be a ready market for all the light emitting diodes they could produce.

A light emitting diode (LED) consists of a semiconductor sandwich that converts electrical energy into light. The main commercial parameter for LEDs is the brightness of the emitted light. In the Litronix process, the LEDs were tested for brightness after the fully manufactured devices were encased in plastic. The completed LEDs were then sorted by brightness and assigned one of several different part numbers. All the devices cost the same to manufacture, but were priced differently: the higher the brightness, the higher the price. Litronix set the lowest price for the least bright devices, but even at this price the profit margin was high. For more demanding applications, there would be brighter devices and the pure upside of even higher margins. It was an industry of the future, poised on the cusp of explosive growth, and Litronix had a winning strategy.

But the product strategy was flawed. As sales of LEDs began to grow, it became apparent that most customers needed high-brightness LEDs. Unfortunately, the company's manufacturing process turned out mostly LEDs of the low-brightness variety. While customers snapped up the high-brightness devices as soon as they came off the line, huge quantities of low-brightness LEDs stacked up in the warehouse. Litronix soon learned there were no high margins to enjoy from sales of premium products unless there were also buyers for the rest of the product line. The obvious solution, to invest time and money revamping its manufacturing process, did not appeal to Litronix. Instead, the company embarked on a considerably more innovative strategy.

In an expansion of its ambition beyond the LED business, beginning with the model 1102 hand-held calculator Litronix entered the consumer products business. The new venture had two compelling arguments in its favor. As a leading manufacturer of LEDs, which in 1972 were a large percentage of the cost of materials in calculators, Litronix would be assured of high profit margins. In addition, as the manufacturer of a high volume product that used even higher volumes of LEDs that didn't have to be particularly bright, Litronix had a captive customer for low-brightness LEDs. It was a brilliant plan. Unfortunately, there was a problem. The Litronix sales organization, built to sell a technical product to original equipment manufacturers, didn't have a clue how to sell a consumer product to a department store. Litronix did not have a channel and no amount of advertising could compensate for it. Eventually, Litronix dropped out of consumer products and returned to its original LED product strategy. However, with its manufacturing issues still unresolved, all it accomplished was to move from a business model where it couldn't sell its products back to a business model where it couldn't make money. In 1979, awash in red ink, Litronix was sold for a very reasonable price to the German technology conglomerate Siemens.

Products are the lifeblood of companies. But as we have seen, the selection of the wrong new product can generate dangerous side effects. If the products do not fit the channel or do not address the needs of the customer base, they will not be sold. If the products have manufacturing issues, they may be sold but not delivered.

And, as in the story of Osborne Computer, even the right new product can be dangerous when introduced in the wrong way. The moral of this story is to make sure you have the right product and take it to market in the right way. It is important for an entrepreneur to think about these types of strategic issues. Do I need a product focus? Do I have a product focus? Is my sales channel able to efficiently take my products to market? Can I make the product I am selling? Can I sell the product I am making? Would I be better off if I reduced my product line, increased my product line, or did neither? You need to consider these types of strategic issues at the earliest stages of your company because you can't get there if you don't know where you are going. It is only after considering the available options and deciding on a strategic direction, that the entrepreneur is ready for the biggest challenge of all: selling something.

CHAPTER SIX

Sales

"When in doubt, tell the truth."
Mark Twain

Sales, the most important subject not taught in business school, is what separates winning companies from the rest of the field. The company with an average product but an excellent sales organization will succeed more often than its competitor with an excellent product but an average sales organization.

In 1981, for example, Osborne Computer chose the Zilog Z-80 as the microcomputer for its revolutionary product the Osborne 1. The Z-80 contained all 78 instructions of the Intel 8080, the highest-selling 8-bit microcomputer at the time, and was compatible with software written for that product. In addition, the Z-80 contained many new instructions that provided additional power and flexibility. Intel's response to the Z-80 was the 8088, a stripped down version of its expensive 16-bit product the 8086, but most industry experts believed even the 8088 fell short against the Z-80. With the best technical solution, Zilog appeared to be poised to win control of the 8-bit microcomputer market. But it didn't happen. Intel responded with aggressive advertising, sales promotions including cash incentives for design wins, and reduced prices for peripheral semiconductor devices when purchased as a "bundle" with the 8088. Intel won the battle and Zilog, in spite of its better product, lost. Today, Zilog continues to manufacture versions of the Z-80 product line and in 2001 posted sales of $172 million, a paltry sum compared to Intel's $26 billion.

The only way to build an outstanding sales organization is to organize your selling activities. One of the most useful tools in this regard is a Sales Pipeline that lists the current status of the identifiable universe of customers and prospects. In the Sales Pipeline, each customer and prospect is identified by stage depending on position in the sales cycle. A current customer that buys and uses the product is termed Stage A; a customer at the product evaluation stage is termed Stage B; an active prospect, meaning the potential customer has been contacted and there is an ongoing discussion, is termed Stage C; and potential customers that have been identified by not yet contacted are termed Stage D. The Sales Pipeline resides in a simple database that can be sorted for various purposes.

For each customer and prospect, the Sales Pipeline of potential annual purchases is adjusted by a "confidence factor" to produce a final value. A Sales Pipeline that is reviewed and updated regularly is an important tool in directing and measuring sales efforts. The bottom line numbers of the Sales Pipeline, however, should not be confused with a sales forecast. While Sales Pipeline numbers are useful from a sales management point of view, they do not constitute a reliable forecast.

Many companies buy a contact management software program to keep track of the sales process. All customer communications, whether by inside sales, outside sales, accounting, or product development, are recorded in the database portion of the software program. The software program is administered from the company's computer network but has extensions that reside on the Sales Representatives' laptop computers. The contents of the laptops are synchronized with the network on a daily basis. The key to making these software programs effective is participation. In my experience, in smaller companies contact management software programs are more trouble than they are worth, but in larger companies the programs can be effective.

However useful Sales Pipelines and imaginative software may be, what's even more important is to assemble a group of competent Sales Representatives who are guided by a management team that understands them. The life of a Sales Representative for an early

Stage	Customer	Product	Units	Price	Gross	Conf	Value
A	Grant Activation	BC-100	400	4	1,600	75%	1,200
A	Mount Forest	BC-200	3,000	6	18,000	60%	10,800
B	Certified	BC-200	250	6	1,500	35%	525
B	Halliday Company	BC-100	2,000	4	8,000	35%	2,800
B	Hitchon Biotech	BC-100	6,000	3	18,000	40%	7,200
B	Kantner Tech	BC-100	70,000	2.6	182,000	30%	54,600
C	Chip Stick	BC-200	12,000	6	72,000	20%	14,400
C	Corbett Industrial	BC-100	2,000	4	8,000	30%	2,400
C	Regis Industries	BC-100	16,000	3.2	51,200	40%	20,480
C	Sheba Biotech	BC-200	100	6	600	5%	30
D	DF Wales	BC-100	500	4	2,000	5%	100
D	Durst Associates	BC-100	500	4	2,000	5%	100
D	Lankin Hellinga	BC-200	1,500	6	9,000	5%	450
D	Schwab	BC-200	1,200	6	7,200	5%	360
D	GG Partners	BC-100	3,000	4	12,000	5%	600
					$393,100		$116,045

Table 2. The Sales Pipeline

stage technology company is no picnic. With a limited base of established customers, most of the Sales Representative's time will be spent "cold calling" on new prospects where merely getting in the door can be a time-consuming process. Once inside, making the sale requires forming a relationship with at least two people, the engineer who makes the technical decision and the buyer who makes the purchasing decision. The needs of these people are quite different. The engineer needs to understand the technical merits of the product. In most cases, additional information and sometimes a sample will be required before coming to a final decision. Only then will the engineer, if the need is current, issue a requisition.

Having secured a requisition, the Sales Representative must now deal with the purchasing department. The buyer rarely responds to a requisition by immediately issuing a purchase order. First, the buyer will want to know if there is a "second source" for the product. If there is a second source, the process may be delayed while a competitive quotation is obtained. If there is no second source, the buyer may contact the engineer and ask for the requisition to be reconsidered, or ask the Sales Representative for Financial Statements or other evidence that the company is financially sound. In any case, during the process from initial sales call until receipt of a purchase order, a period of several months or more can elapse during which the Sales Representative will have made dozens of trips and telephone calls chasing down this single order. The job of management is to provide support though building a sales culture with defined procedures and expectations, and continuous reinforcement through personal encouragement, communications, and close supervision including participation in sales calls.

Many companies try to add new customers by energizing Sales Representatives with programs and contests. But the strategy doesn't work. Left to their own devices, Sales Representatives have neither the incentives nor the tools to accomplish the job. From their point of view, prospecting for new accounts is a waste of time. It is also, from the point of view of management, an inefficient process. Identification of new customers is far better left to the inside sales staff. The procedure involves developing a profile of the attributes of a potential new customer, then generating a list of prospects for each geographic area. Next, purchasing and/or product development managers at the prospect companies are interviewed by telephone, and contact sheets are compiled. As an inducement to the inside sales staff, a small commission should be paid for each completed contact sheet and a larger commission when a prospect is subsequently converted into a customer.

Effective sales management consists of equal parts encouragement and discipline. The encouragement part is easy and the discipline part is hard. Sales Representatives are motivated by the prospect of personal success, and they tend to pursue whatever is in their self-interest. Think of them as junior entrepreneurs. It is no simple matter to impose a set of rules upon individuals with such finely developed personalities, but the task is not impossible. What is needed is an alignment of the rules with the self-interest. The best policy is to couple compensation of Sales Representatives with the selling activities that will most help the company to achieve its sales forecast. A growth company should pay commissions mostly on design-wins and increases in business, because selling to new customers and selling more to existing customers are more valuable to the company, and more difficult for the Sales Representatives, than maintaining the *status quo* of existing relationships.

Nevertheless, most companies compensate their Sales Representatives based on total sales in a geographic territory. The practice sets the company up for future problems. The day will come when sales flatten out because the Sales Representative has reached a personal limit of capacity. At that time, management is faced with the unhappy choice of keeping the Sales Representative and accepting lower than possible sales or firing the Sales Representative and putting existing business at risk. A much better strategy, the one advocated above, is to compensate Sales Representatives in a manner that will not restrict your ability to take advantage of future opportunities: base compensation on the quality of the selling activity rather than the quantity.

A well-managed sales organization can be expanded into new geographic territories by hiring qualified people and slotting them into the existing system. But even after the country has been blanketed from coast to coast with Sales Representatives, there are still more green pastures available. A company with products that derive value from intellectual property, the proper definition of every technology company, should find a demand for its products throughout the world. Most products sold in the United States can certainly be sold in Canada and Europe, and probably can be sold in Japan, China and Korea.

The international market is relatively easy and inexpensive to access. Distributors, the usual Canadian and European channel, buy the product at a discount of about 30% and resell it to their customers in the local currency. A distributor usually carries inventory and publishes its own marketing materials. A distributor has the built-in advantage of assuming the end customer collections risk. An independent representative is the usual channel in Japan, China, Korea and other countries with complicated import-export procedures or currency restrictions. Commission rates are typically 10-15% of sales. Shipments are made directly to the end customer and the company bears the accounts receivable risk. Offsetting this risk is the usual practice of requiring payment by letter of credit, a financial instrument that virtually assures payment.

Through careful attention to the sales process including the continuous identification of new customers, close management of Sales Representatives, and expansion into new geographical markets, an early stage technology company can generate an increasing flow of new orders. The generation of new orders, however, is not an end in itself. Orders mean nothing without the ability to profitably fulfill them. That's the next part of our story.

CHAPTER SEVEN

Management and the WAR Report

*"People who work sitting down get paid more
than people who work standing up."*
Ogden Nash

An early stage technology company is not a democracy. It is
your responsibility alone to decide the direction of the company
and to allocate its precious resources. At the same time, your
managers and supervisors need to make, and assume a personal
responsibility for, independent decisions. It's a delicate balancing
act and to successfully pull it off requires the right chemistry between
the entrepreneur and the staff. By chemistry, I do not mean your
staff should be naturally subservient. On the contrary, staff members
should have their own opinions that they are unafraid to voice.
Your part of the equation is to listen carefully and, should the new
idea be better than your old one, to acknowledge the fact, thank
the person, and change your mind.

The most efficient way to build a team with the right chemistry
is to do the hiring yourself. I believe the entrepreneur should
personally hire the company's first 25 employees or, at the very
least, should personally hire managers and supervisors. Having
stressed the importance of chemistry, it is also important to stress
the importance of knowledge and experience. No amount of
chemistry can compensate for incompetence. As a general rule,
hire strangers and beware of relatives, friends, and relatives of friends.
Do your own recruiting. Find management through referrals from
people you know and respect. For technicians and office help, the
best way to generate a pile of resumes is to run an inexpensive

"help wanted" ad in the local newspaper. If you plan to hire scientists or engineers, ads in college newspapers and postings on appropriate web sites can generate good results.

Your lawyer will prepare an Offer of Employment that you can modify with the specific information for each person hired. Make sure the document includes language to protect the proprietary commercial information of the company, specifies intellectual property developed by an employee is owned by the company, and obligates the employee to execute any necessary documents to assign and maintain the company's intellectual property even after he or she has ceased to be an employee. In addition, include language that prohibits disclosure of salary or Stock Options (in the event the company issues them in the future) to any third party except to a spouse or financial advisor.

One final point on the subject of hiring: except when absolutely necessary, try to avoid recruiting employees from outside the immediate area. There are three main issues. First of all the relocation costs will be higher and more varied than you think: the cost of the moving van is only the beginning. Second, in order to recruit the individual whose services you think you so desperately need, you will probably pay too high a salary in relation to existing employees and sow the seeds of future discontent. Third, even if you transformed a junior engineer from Iowa into a senior engineer in California, the new employee frequently will become dissatisfied and, as the number of relocated family members increases, so does the probability of dissatisfaction.

Having recruited a staff, it is time to lead them in the right direction. During the working week, you will have ample opportunities to personally communicate with each member of your staff. In addition to "management by walking around," it is also necessary to communicate in a more structured environment. I prefer to schedule weekly management meetings every Monday morning, beginning an hour before the usual start time, and with the sole agenda item being a discussion of the Weekly Activity Report. I first learned of this report from a venture capitalist named Richard Black who calls it, somewhat redundantly, the WAR Report.

Week ending:	*29-Nov*	*6-Dec*	*13-Dec*	*20-Dec*
Billings	6	9	12	4
New Orders	9	15	8	1
Backlog	9	15	11	8
Book-to-Bill Ratio (4 wks)	1.23	1.48	1.15	1.06
Cash	106	100	98	94
Cash Flow	-5	-6	-6	-4
Accounts Receivable	38	41	47	47
Accounts Payable	3	4	4	6
Inventory:				
Raw Materials	8	7	7	12
Finished Goods	0	3	0	0
Rework Rate	2.10%	1.80%	0.70%	1.40%
Capital Purchases	0	1	0	0
Headcount	5	5	5	5
New Sales Leads	9	2	7	3
New Accounts	1	0	0	2

Table 3. The WAR Report

The great advantage of the WAR Report is it reflects the current situation. In order for financial statistics to be useful to operational management, they must be in real time. For example, it might be interesting for management to read the monthly Financial Statements and learn that inventories increased by $10,000 in the month that ended four weeks previously, but such knowledge is of little use. However, management can do something about the fact that inventories today are $5,000 higher than last week.

The WAR Report contains more financial information than managers receive at most companies. But the way I look at it, show me a manager who cannot benefit from knowing the actual financial position of the company and I'll show you someone who shouldn't be a manager. At the beginning, you will be the only person in the room who appreciates the relevance of each line item, but that will change sooner than you think. Before long, every manager is going to understand a great deal about the larger picture and why his or her individual contribution is important. Knowledge is empowering. When management has a powerful understanding of the company's business, it will also have the confidence to make good decisions.

Because the company is in business of selling, the WAR Report begins with the weekly progress report of sales: Billings, New Orders, Backlog and the Book-to-Bill Ratio. For the most recent week, Billings of $4,000 is the total amount of product shipped and invoiced to customers during the week. During the week, the company received $1,000 in New Orders, and the week ended with a Backlog of $8,000. The Book-to-Bill ratio compares New Orders to Billings over a four-week period, and a value higher than unity is indicative of growth.

Some of the facts and figures in the WAR Report will be of limited interest to the group as a whole, but even so, everything is important. The discussion of the WAR Report will address the underlying issues reflected by the statistics and what, if anything, can be done to improve performance. In addition, managers need visibility into the consequences of operations, especially the current status of the most important measurement of a technology company's financial health: its Cash Flow.

CHAPTER EIGHT

Cash Flow

"To get back on your feet, miss two car payments."
Anonymous

Cash flow problems are like human illnesses. Some strike during periods of growth, for example when a business expansion takes longer than expected or the introduction of a new product ends in failure. Like childhood diseases, companies that survive these rites of passage are usually stronger for it. There are also cash flow problems similar to the flu. These infect a sizeable portion of the corporate population whenever there is a downturn in the general economy. Other cash flow problems, like diabetes, target an at-risk population, and are a continuing threat to companies overexposed to risk. These three types of cash flow problems can be quite dangerous, even terminal, but they also have a quality that can be a saving grace. They are predictable. It is managements' responsibility to anticipate and be prepared to deal with such events. However, cash flow problems can also arise out of the blue. Like a sudden heart attack in a seemingly healthy person, these entirely unpredictable cash flow problems can be especially dangerous.

For example, while I was president of CRS Robotics Corporation, an unpredictable and serious cash flow problem was caused by grease. A few months previously, the manufacturer of the grease that lubricated the "joints" of our robots had changed the formulation. The manufacturer's specifications for the new grease were identical to the old grease, but the new grease performed differently in our robots. After a few hundred hours of operation, the new grease became slightly less viscous and leaked out of the joints. With the robot arm moving back and forth at high speed, grease was splattered over a wide area. Because our robots were used mostly in clean environments such as pharmaceutical laboratories, robots that splattered grease were completely unacceptable to our customers.

After the introduction of the new grease into production, there was a two-month period of business as usual during which everything we built and shipped was defective. Then, quite suddenly, we had a big problem. There were dozens of angry customers, invoices were not being paid, and production had ground to a halt. At the time, I didn't view the situation as a cash flow problem. It was a production problem that our engineers understood and knew how to solve. I knew it would take time to locate a new source of grease that would perform suitably in our application, and also understood there would be financial issues in the interim, but, comfortable in the knowledge that fixing the grease problem would fix everything else, that's what I concentrated on.

Final assembly was shut down, but the incoming pace of new orders continued at the normal rate and the backlog steadily grew. We instructed production to manufacture sub-assemblies that could quickly be built into finished robots when the new grease became available. Cash was scarce and revenues had been reduced to a trickle, but once we obtained supplies of the new grease, our troubles would be over. As soon as we could send technicians into the field to change out the old grease with the new, the cash would begin to flow, and with large numbers of robots coming off the production line, we would make up the lost business in an orgy of shipments. Unfortunately, the solution of the problem was easier to intellectualize than to implement.

When management confronts a difficult problem, it usually understands what needs to be done and is able to put together a workable plan. And so did we, but we were a little off on the timing. It took twelve weeks—three full months of unrelenting expenses and reduced revenues—to finally resolve the grease problem. If the company's balance sheet and relationship with the bank had been a little less strong, or if it had taken much more than twelve weeks to resume shipments, the company may not have survived. In retrospect, the appropriate response to the grease problem would have been to focus on cash management and to reduce expenses to a sustainable level until the problem was solved.

When addressing a serious cash flow problem, implementing the obvious operational solution is the first inclination of management. However, more often than not the operational problem requires too much time to be corrected. Time, not business efficiency, is the enemy. With business in a tailspin, if the operational problem remains unresolved while the outward flow of cash continues unabated, at some point the downward trajectory may become unstoppable. In these situations, cash is more important than performance.

The first time I faced a serious cash flow problem, I knew none of this. Luckily, I had a partner named Norm MacPhail. Norm was a minority owner when Varah Electronics hired me as a salesman, but by 1980 we were equal partners. In the previous three years, we had bought out the other shareholders, tripled annual revenues to more than twelve million dollars and expanded the business from a single location with thirty employees and five hundred customers, to four locations with one hundred employees and several thousand customers. The expansion had been financed by debt. We owed six hundred thousand dollars to the former owners. If the company failed to make monthly interest payments, the debt could be converted back into shares and the former owners would regain control of the company. There were also bank term loans totaling a few hundred thousand dollars that were secured by the company's fixed assets. The remaining assets of the company, in particular accounts receivable and inventory, were pledged as security for a three million dollar bank credit line, and the credit line was also secured by our personal guarantees. In total, Norm and I owed about four million dollars.

Varah Electronics sold electronic components such as integrated circuits, resistors and connectors, to industrial companies, governments and educational institutions. The company was an authorized distributor for about one hundred component manufacturers. Between the four stocking locations, component inventories included over five thousand different part numbers that were purchased in bulk and sold in smaller quantities to a large number of customers. The average gross margin was about 28%. However, after deducting expenses, interest costs and taxes, only a few percent remained as net profit. During the previous three years, net profits had decreased from about 4% to less than 2% due to startup expenses for the new locations and higher interest rates.

Distribution is a low margin business, but it can have the compensating advantage of stability. In our case, most of our customers were large, credit-worthy industrial companies, governments and educational institutions. For the most part, these organizations purchased our products for repair and maintenance purposes, activities that are relatively independent of the ups and downs of the general economy. With a predictable top line and steady customers who paid their bills, Varah Electronics was basically solid. The thin bottom line was the only aspect of the business in need of improvement.

The bottom line problem was primarily the result of high interest rates, and we expected it to resolve itself in the near future. During the previous three years, the prime rate had risen from six to twelve percent. A few years previously, the prime rate has also risen from six to twelve percent. That time, due to the OPEC energy crisis, it took three years before rates fell back. This time, without a definable economic crisis to prolong the situation, economists expected interest rates to fall back to a reasonable level even faster.

But the economists were wrong. Instead of dropping, interest rates moved in the opposite direction. The prime rate hit an historic high of 20% in April 1980. Economists considered the situation to be a temporary aberration, and this time they were right. In three months the prime rate plunged nine points to 11%. However, six months of astronomical interest rates had put us in the red and the bank was in the process of reevaluating our credit facility. Somehow Norm kept the bank on side and dealt with their concerns until September 1980 when, after posting our third consecutive month of profitability, the pressure from the bank eased off. We were definitely back on track. Norm and I, but especially Norm because finance was his responsibility, breathed a sigh of relief that the so-called "classical interest rate spike" had run its course.

Unfortunately, our enthusiasm for the future was premature. Rather than continuing on its widely forecasted slide back to earth, by the end of 1980 the prime rate had shot back up by more than ten percent into the stratosphere of 21½%. Even worse, this was no interest rate spike. For almost two years, the prime rate did not venture south of 15%, our days of profitability faded into memory, and the company remained continuously short of cash due to high interest rates. High interest rates also had a negative impact on our customers that resulted in lower sales and slower collections, but equally serious was the effect on average selling prices. As competition for business in a declining market increased, month-by-month profit margins eroded and losses mounted until the continued existence of the company was in jeopardy.

We were in survival mode. Norm's job was to cut expenses, manage our cash, and keep the bank on side. My job was to increase sales in spite of the declining market, and if possible to keep margins high, but in any event to generate sufficient dollars in gross margin to reduce losses to a sustainable level. A truism that venture capitalists are fond of repeating, the wisdom of which I have since come to appreciate, is that you cannot sell your way out of trouble. That was exactly my assignment and I embraced the challenge in blissful ignorance.

For some years I credited my accomplishments during this period to personal ability, but in hindsight I was simply in the right place at the right time. The microcomputer revolution had just begun and my company was an authorized distributor for most of the major component manufacturers including Motorola, National, RCA, Texas Instruments, and most importantly of all, Intel. Microcomputer components were suddenly in tremendous demand. As one of the few suppliers of these products, we regularly received urgent telephone calls from equipment manufacturers across the country and as far away as Europe and Japan. To keep their production lines running, these companies were prepared to pay a premium price and, even more significantly from the point of view of cash flow, they paid cash on delivery. During most of 1981, as sales to regular customers decreased and margins continued to shrink, we made up most of the shortfall by selling microcomputer components to far-flung manufacturers with urgent needs. Then, at the end of 1981, additional capacity at the semiconductor companies came on-line and this lucrative market dried. Fortunately for us, however, as the one opportunistic market shut down, one step up the microcomputer food chain another market opened up.

In 1983, Osborne Computer encountered its own cash crunch of monumental proportions that led to its bankruptcy, but in 1982 the company was flying high. Osborne's computer systems were in great demand and extremely scarce, and we were one of the few suppliers. And this time there was an added bonus. Not only were customers willing to pay cash, they were also willing to place a 50% deposit to get on the waiting list. Deposits merely accumulate on the balance sheet and have no impact on profit and loss, but deposits have a tremendous impact on cash flow. During most of 1982, our cash flow was bolstered by hundreds of thousands of dollars in deposits.

By generating opportunistic sales and garnering customer deposits, I made an important contribution to our lengthy battle for survival, but the work was not particularly difficult. Norm's job was far more demanding. Not only did he have to make up the balance of the cash shortfall by cutting expenses, but he also had to collect receivables, push out payables, control inventory, and manage the expectations of employees, customers and suppliers. At the same time, and by far the most challenging task of all, Norm had to sustain the continued support of the bank. The amount of money we were authorized to borrow was calculated each month based on the status of our inventory and accounts receivable. On several occasions, the margin calculation put us over the limit and in grave danger of having the loan called, but each time Norm persuaded the bank to provide a temporary overdraft to cover the shortfall.

For two years, I sold and Norm did everything else. I was constantly on the road and Norm was always in his office. When the door was shut, he was on the telephone providing comfort to the bank, convincing customers to pay sooner, cajoling suppliers to wait a little longer, or helping the branch managers resolve their problems. When his door was open, it was an invitation for employees to drop in and unload their problems. Norm did not believe in memos, but was always willing to talk.

Norm was a self-taught man who went to sea as a teenager and became a radio operator in the merchant service during World War Two. After the war, he spent a few years as a commercial fisherman until a telephone company hired him as a radio engineer. Norm had no formal education in engineering, but he excelled at the job. His last position before joining Varah Electronics was as regional manager for the telecommunications company Marconi. He had no formal business education either but, again, he excelled at the job. It was there, at Marconi, that Norm learned to manage cash.

Cash flow problems impacted every facet of our business. As the months of unrelentingly high interest rates dragged on, it became progressively more challenging to collect accounts receivable. Everybody—customers, suppliers, competitors—were squeezed for cash. It became increasingly difficult to make up arrears in receivables by pushing out payables because important suppliers began to demand payment within terms. The penalty for an overdue invoice was cessation of all shipments. Because many of these shipments went directly into the lucrative cash sales channel we had come to depend upon, it was necessary to pay invoices to certain suppliers within terms no matter what. In addition, there was the additional complication of rampant inflation that drove every line item on the expense statement higher and higher.

Interest rates finally began to come down in the final months of 1982. By February 1983, the prime rate had plunged to 10½% and after two difficult years the business crisis was finally over. But it had not happened soon enough. The demanding and stressful job that Norm performed so well had a tragic impact on his health. By the middle of 1982, with the prime still above the 15% mark, Norm was diagnosed with inoperable brain cancer. He died in December of 1982, leaving a widow and three teenage children. Norm was capable, unassuming, honest, a good friend, and I miss him to this day.

ooo

The rewards of careful cash management are not infinite, but they are substantial. Compared to an average technology company, one with excellent cash management may have enough extra cash to cover a month's payroll for its salaried employees. That's an operational cushion worth the effort. The key to excellent cash management is controlling the cash flowing out of the business through attention to accounts payable, and controlling cash flowing into the business through attention to accounts receivable. The cash flowing out of the business is, of course, completely under your control and relatively easy to manage. The other side of the equation, however, is seemingly outside your control and difficult to manage. But appearances can be deceiving.

A useful perspective from which to consider the subject of collecting receivables is the point of view of your customers. To them, the issue is managing payables and there is a three-tier pecking order that determines which bills get paid first. At the highest level are those bills that always get paid on time such as taxes, payroll, and payroll withholdings. The reason these are paid within terms is that failure to do so results in the most severe penalties. The second group of obligations includes loan payments, utilities and rent. Failure to pay these bills within terms can result in unpleasant consequences, but no jail time. At the lowest tier, in terms of payment priority, are ordinary vendors. In short, your receivables are among your customers' least urgent financial obligations. Even so, companies do not pay all ordinary vendors the same. Think of you own payables—for various reasons there are certain vendors that need to be paid on time. The same reasoning applies to your customers.

At Tm Bioscience Corporation there were many vendors of laboratory supplies and reagents but some got paid sooner than others. Four, in particular, come to mind. One was so persistent in its collections procedures that our accounts payable clerk, rather than deal with the hassle, processed their invoices with priority. Another was a supplier that was conveniently located. Our scientists and laboratory technicians came to rely on this vendor because they could pop over and pick up needed items immediately. The third vendor that was paid with priority was a supplier of synthetic DNA. We had many such vendors, but this one supplied products of such consistently high quality that our scientists insisted on purchasing synthetic DNA for certain applications from this particular source. The fourth vendor supplied custom reagents for a particular laboratory instrument. We had no choice but to purchase these reagents from this sole-source supplier, and, when asked, we paid this vendor's invoices within terms. However, most of the time the vendor didn't ask and was therefore rarely paid within terms.

Most invoices issued by most companies are due 30 days after the date of the invoice, and most companies pay their trade payables on average about 15 to 30 days *after* the due date. If a company paid all its trade suppliers within invoice terms, the fact would be immediately apparent to the Board of Directors during the quarterly process of approving the company's financial statements. If this hypothetical scenario was ever to occur, and to my knowledge it never has, it would be considered grounds for dismissal of the boss. In the real world, the only obligations that are always settled within terms are those that must be paid on time. The rest, except for priority vendors and those with persistent collections, are paid about 60 days after the invoice date.

In addition to positioning your company, if possible, as a vendor whose invoices need to be treated with priority, and in any case as a vendor with a persistent collections procedure, there are a few other things to consider that help minimize the delay between issuing an invoice and receiving payment. First of all, the sooner a company invoices, the sooner it is paid. Most customers pay invoices a certain number of days after the date of the invoice, in which case invoices dated Friday are paid three days sooner than invoices dated Monday. Companies that invoice on the day of shipment get paid sooner than companies that do not. The identical logic applies to companies that have streamlined their internal order fulfillment procedures. Companies requiring orders to be filled and shipped the same day get paid sooner than companies that do not. At Varah Electronics, for example, at one time the shipping department was accumulating small shipments into larger shipments in order to reduce freight costs to the customer. Some of these small shipments were being held for weeks or more. The shipping procedure, long ignored by management, resulted in savings for our customers but it hurt our cash flow. We changed the shipping policy.

Many companies seek to improve their collections by offering discounts for prompt payment. In my experience, this strategy is rarely effective and frequently results in many customers taking the discount for prompt payment even when they have not paid the invoice within the terms. In a few situations, such as when a particular customer is known to reliably pay within the stated terms, the strategy can be beneficial. Usually, however, this approach of using a carrot for prompt payment is only reliable if there is also a stick. At Varah Electronics, for example, certain major semiconductor manufacturers offered a 1% discount for payment within terms and made it clear that authorized distributors who did not take the discount placed their franchise in jeopardy. Even if you do not offer discounts for prompt payment, make sure you include a provision for "negative discounts" in the legal boilerplate printed on your invoices. The language invokes the legal right to charge interest on overdue accounts. The language, even if the company does not routinely enforce it, can sometimes make it easier to collect problem accounts.

A final procedural issue is that of statements. The only beneficiaries of statements are late-paying customers. To them, statements provide a convenient excuse: "I'm sorry, but those invoices cannot be paid until the statement is reconciled." If you produce statements, stop. Not only will collections improve, but you will also save postage and the costs associated with generating, filing and keeping track of them. When customers ask for statements, the best response is to explain that the company does not generate statements but can provide a list of outstanding invoices. List the invoices from the oldest to the most recent in a single document that is not divided into time periods.

Most companies have a standardized procedure to collect overdue accounts. Historically, the collections process began with a written demand for payment that included copies of overdue invoices hand-stamped "Past Due" in red ink. This labor-intensive start remains standard practice in many companies, and evidence of the practice can be found in the self-inking stamp aisle of any office supply store in the country. It was probably effective in those bygone days when every company had a legion of office workers who meticulously attended to the administration of correspondence. But it doesn't work any longer. Companies that begin their collections procedure with written communications are wasting their money and, more importantly from the point of view of cash flow, are needlessly prolonging the process of collecting receivables by days or weeks.

Today, the procedure of collecting receivables does not begin until the first telephone call is made. In many circumstances there will be written correspondence flowing back and forth between the vendor and the customer, but the documents are subordinate to the verbal communications between individuals. The most important factor in collections is personal communication. Communications should be between Victoria and Jim, not between Consolidated Supply Company and International Widget Corporation. It follows that the ability to communicate is the most important job qualification for the accounts receivable clerk. It is also necessary for this individual to be reasonably proficient in math, able to maintain accurate records, and capable of working long hours in a repetitive job, but without the outgoing personality of a communicator the person will be unable to perform his or her job at a high level. In addition, effective collections personnel tend to be somewhat bureaucratic with a streak of righteousness. These attributes allow the individual to be comfortable in a job that requires management authorization for anything out of the ordinary, and also to keep a positive attitude during a working day of verbal skirmishing with strangers.

When collecting receivables, you occupy the ethical high ground. You are not "asking for something" because that implies there is some question of entitlement. The facts of the situation and the rights of the parties should never be placed in doubt. It is a simple matter of commercial law. The buyer and seller entered into a contractual relationship defined by purchase orders and invoices. As promised by the seller, the product or service has been supplied, but payment for the product or service has not been made as promised by the buyer. These are the unspoken facts. In addition to the unspoken legal obligations of the customer, comments that do not directly relate to the purpose of the call should also be left unsaid. Similarly, the natural instinct to justify one's actions must be suppressed. A remark such as "We have a cash flow problem and have made the collection of overdue accounts a priority" can have unintended consequences that can be quite severe.

At Varah Electronics, for example, a long-time customer switched suppliers shortly after we put a major push on collections. Thinking the customer was offended by our new, more aggressive collections procedures, I visited the general manager to try to patch things up. I was told the company had switched suppliers after someone in our receivables department insisted on prompt payment because we were having financial difficulties. The general manager explained that, even though our companies had enjoyed a good relationship for many years, they had no choice but to change vendors because a reliable source of supply was essential to their business. It took more than three years to win this customer back.

The collections procedure begins with an aged accounts receivable listing. Most business accounting software packages allow this information to be viewed on-line or to be printed with various amounts of detail and in different formats. My preference, and that of every receivables clerk I know, is to work from a paper copy that can be marked up during the collections process. The document lists customers in alphabetical order and summarizes the total amount owed by each, and sub-totals of the amount that is outstanding but current (not yet due for payment), the amount overdue by less than 30 days, the amount overdue by 30-60 days, and the amount overdue by more than 60 days. Beneath these summaries, all outstanding invoices are listed in order from the oldest to the most recent, with dividing lines separating the aging periods: over 60 days, 30-60 days, less than 30 days, and current.

Besides these basic data, it is useful to have additional collections-specific information in the accounts receivable listing that can be entered and updated by the accounts receivable clerk. This information will include the customer's mail and courier delivery address, accounts payable contact name, telephone, fax, email, and an area for ongoing notes and a description of the customer's internal payables procedures. How do they process payables? Do they have regular check runs and, if so, how often? Who has the authority to approve checks for payment? In some organizations, payment is approved by the individual who issued the requisition, and in other companies by the purchasing supervisor or department manager. How many people within the company are authorized to sign checks? The more you know about a customer's internal procedures, the easier the process of collections becomes because the receivables clerk is able to make specific requests and the receivables supervisor will be able to provide better advice about strategies to use with a particular customer. Having this information in a single document is most convenient, however, some accounting software packages do not provide this level of flexibility. In such cases, the additional information can be maintained in a separate file.

Like all office jobs, collections work has its share of repetitive activities that can become routine, but unlike most office jobs, these activities are rarely boring. In fact, the job continually deals with new situations that can be very difficult to tactfully resolve, especially since the collections clerk has limited authority to commit the resources of the company. For new clerks, job-related stress can be reduced, and performance enhanced, by thoroughly discussing the nature of collections work and providing realistic training such as role-playing. In addition, an experienced supervisor should sit with an inexperienced clerk during the first few hours of collections work to provide real-time encouragement and support.

The most effective method of collecting receivables is quite simple. The keys to success are polite insistence and sustained persistence. It is an iterative process in which the clerk methodically works his or her way through the aged accounts receivable listing in a series of passes. Some customers will require multiple telephone calls to resolve various issues such as missing paperwork. Others will be difficult, sometimes bordering on impossible, to contact. In these cases, leave a message or voice mail. Ask that your call be returned by a specific time. If the call is not returned on time, phone back. If the person is not available, first ask if Ralph or Mary is in the building and then ask for the party to be paged. If there is no response to the page, speak to the accounting supervisor. Tell the supervisor you need to speak with Ralph and ask for help tracking him down. It may take many consecutive days of following this course of sustained persistence, but eventually your contact will be more easily accessible and, providing you are insistently polite, over time an acceptable working relationship will develop.

As you work through the list for the first time from A to Z, take detailed notes including all promises made by the customer because the process is driven by commitments made by one individual to another. These personal commitments are more compelling, in terms of extracting payment, than the legal obligations of the original transaction. Soliciting commitments and following up on them are the most powerful weapons in your arsenal.

Begin the first telephone conversation with a question about the oldest outstanding invoice. "I am phoning about your account. What is the status of invoice 3458?" You are not asking for payment, you are courteously establishing the expectation of payment with a question that leaves many issues unstated. Rather than start in with a demand for payment of an overdue invoice, you have merely inquired about the status of the invoice. Collections work is most effective when there is a non-confrontational relationship between the parties. Ralph has never heard of invoice 3458 and will respond with a question. Whatever his response, your goal during this first telephone call is to keep the conversation going while you establish the necessary preconditions that allow you to ask a very specific question, "Will invoice 3458 be paid this week?" You need to tell Ralph, or even better maneuver the conversation in such a way that he tells you, that the invoice is valid and it is overdue for payment. When you have laid the groundwork and finally pop the question, Ralph's response is a personal commitment. Write it down. I recommend restricting this first telephone call to obtaining a commitment on the single most overdue invoice, and steering clear of larger issues. The goal of the first telephone call is to obtain this one personal commitment that will become a template for the relationship: you call, he makes a commitment, you follow up.

The second and subsequent series of calls will introduce more invoices for which you seek a personal commitment. During these rounds of telephone calls, the aged receivables listing should be worked according to priority rather than in alphabetical order. In my opinion, the priority should be the accounts most likely to pay. This is exactly opposite the conventional wisdom that you should concentrate your efforts on the most egregiously overdue accounts. My reason is simple: if the point of the exercise is to generate cash in the shortest possible period of time, and it is, then it is counterproductive to wait until the end of the process to contact those customers most likely to pay. Studies have shown that the greatest improvement in collections is achieved by targeting accounts that are 0-30 days overdue. For the most part, these are due by customers with the money to pay and the desire to meet their financial obligations.

After several weeks and a half-dozen trips through the accounts receivable listing, most accounts will be in reasonable shape and the focus of most collections activity will be addressing receivables as soon as they become due. In between each round of collections activity, the results should be discussed with the accounts receivable supervisor. This individual may be the controller, CFO or entrepreneur, but in any case will be able to provide advice about future tactics and make decisions that are outside the authority of the receivables clerk.

For example, the supervisor can arrange for sales personnel or a manager to pick up checks at the customer's offices on the promised date, or consent to a series of post-dated checks according to a negotiated schedule authorized by management. A telephone call from one Chief Executive Officer to another can sometimes do wonders, and there is always the option of withholding shipments. This can be particularly effective if your company is the sole-source supplier. For accounts that are problematical, for example at risk of bankruptcy, the supervisor might authorize a return. It's better to have the product back than to incur a bad debt. If the product is saleable at full price, all that has been lost is the profit margin on the original deal. There is also the possibility of accepting payment in kind if the customer is also a supplier, or making other special deals. For example, the supervisor might be able to arrange for selected good customers to pay their entire account—both current and overdue invoices—in return for a discount.

Maintaining an efficient collections process requires polite insistence and sustained persistence on the part of the receivables clerk, and diligent supervision by management, but it is not a fundamentally difficult process. So long as customers and suppliers need each other, they will usually do whatever is necessary to resolve issues between them. Sometimes, however, the usual symbiotic relationship of companies that do business together is not enough to convince the buyer to pay for the products or services that have been legally supplied. In these cases, many companies turn to collection agencies. These outside service providers usually charge 25-50% of the amount they collect. In my opinion, however, there is nothing they can do that you cannot do for yourself. If an agency can collect an overdue account, so can you.

Sometimes, a problem customer will pay less than the amount due with a check that has been endorsed "payment in full." Rather than depositing such a check, it is better to get your lawyer involved. You need legal advice. In some cases, the check can be deposited after appending the words "without prejudice" to the body of the check. In other cases, depending on the circumstances and the jurisdiction, regardless of how your have endorsed the check you may lose the right to pursue payment of the balance by the act depositing the check. Depending on the financial strength of the customer and the size of the discount taken, sometimes it's better to return the check. Besides dealing with endorsed checks, there are a number of other situations where it may be prudent to get your lawyer involved.

There is nothing worse than a bad debt. You not only lose the cash, but the full amount is a hit to profitability. One way to reduce bad debts is to require a customer to sign an agreement prior to shipment, for example a promissory note that places the vendor in a secured position. Another technique is to obtain a personal guarantee from an officer of the debtor company. It is also possible to ship certain types of goods, for example a piece of equipment, under a contract that specifies legal title does not pass until the invoice is paid in full. Whenever it is possible to obtain additional security, do so. In the event of a bankruptcy or receivership, with appropriate security in place you will be paid in full before unsecured creditors receive any payment at all. These methods are realistic options for high value transactions and in special circumstances, for example when a customer requests its credit limit to be increased to a level that that would not otherwise be acceptable, but involving your lawyer to obtain additional security prior to shipment is impractical in most business situations.

For most companies, lawyers are not routinely involved in the sales process but do have an occasional role to play in collections. For example, when a customer files for bankruptcy protection, it may be possible to reclaim title to products already shipped by demanding their return within a short period of time such as ten days. The demand must be made within a specified period of time or you forever lose the right to demand the return of your goods. In it is also necessary to file a proof of claim that establishes your right to participate in whatever distribution of funds may eventually be made to unsecured creditors. This document must be submitted in the proper legal format, and also within a limited period of time. Due to these and other time constraints of the process, it is essential to immediately obtain legal advice whenever a customer files for bankruptcy protection.

It is far better, obviously, to prevent a bad debt rather than deal with it. Your lawyer can provide help in this regard, too, but you need to carefully assess the situation before invoking it. In my opinion, even though a large number of lawyers offer the service, a law firm should not be used as a collection agency. The appropriate role for lawyers in the collections process is only in those cases where the vendor is prepared to take legal action if required.

Without the resolve to follow up with a lawsuit, the strategy of sending a "warning letter" on law firm stationary can be a waste of time and money. There are three possible outcomes to sending a warning letter that you do not intend to back up with legal action. If the delinquent customer believes it has a legal reason not to pay, it will either ignore the warning or have its law firm send a response. Since you have already decided not to follow up with a lawsuit, the warning letter will have no impact other than to convert a problem account into a permanently uncollectable account. The second possible outcome also results in nonpayment, but in this case the customer does not have a legitimate reason for withholding payment. All the warning letter accomplishes is to place the issue back into your court. However, since you have already decided not to follow up with a lawsuit, the process has nowhere to go and the outstanding account will probably never be paid. The third possible outcome is payment of the outstanding amount. This is a good thing, but it also raises the possibility that the customer was willing to pay and might have done so with a little more in-house effort. In other words, the outstanding amount was probably collectable in the traditional fashion, and possibly sooner, but certainly less expensively.

It is, however, appropriate and cost effective to direct your lawyer to send a warning letter to a delinquent customer who adamantly refuses to pay for reasons you believe to be invalid, or a seriously delinquent long-term problem account that is completely unresponsive. In either case, the warning letter must be backed up a carefully considered decision to take any additional necessary legal action. The most important factor in coming to this decision is the customer's ability to pay. If the customer has pockets of sufficient depth, discuss what you believe to be the strength of your case with your lawyer. If your case is not strong, consider negotiating a settlement for less than the outstanding amount as an alternative to legal action.

Sometimes, a lawsuit results in quick payment but more frequently it does not. Legal action can be expensive and time-consuming, and is only appropriate as a final resort. The procedure is even more expensive if you customer is out-of-state and it becomes necessary to recruit a second lawyer from that jurisdiction. Rather than face the high cost of litigation, an increasing number of companies with commercial disputes are resolving their differences through binding arbitration. For those companies that elect to go to court, a steady outflow of cash can accelerate into a torrent once the process shifts into high gear with motions, discovery and trial. Eventually, the court will come to a decision, but sometimes the expenses don't stop and you don't get your money. Instead, you get a piece of paper called a judgment. With this piece of paper in hand, your lawyer can direct the sheriff to seize assets that can be sold to satisfy the judgment, or place a lien against real estate. It can take a fair amount of time to convert seized assets into cash and an indeterminate amount of time to collect against the lien. When the lien will be satisfied is dictated by circumstances outside your control, for example the need to establish clear title prior to obtaining a mortgage on the property.

CHAPTER NINE

Product Development

*"Nearly every one who develops and idea works at it up to the point
where it looks impossible, and then gets discouraged.
That's not the place to become discouraged."*

Thomas Edison

Of the two terms applied to the creative process in a technology
company, I prefer "product development" rather than "research
and development" because the goal of the activity is to develop
products, and the achievement of goals can be encouraged through
terminology. The difference between "research" and "development"
is the former is about creating new science and it is fun, but the
latter is about applying existing technologies and it is work. The
proper place for basic research, the exploration of fundamental
science without a preconceived goal, is the university. So-called
applied research, conducted within a predefined scientific area, is
the charter of governmental research institutions and is also an
appropriate activity for large corporations. But in any case, an early
stage technology company cannot afford to fund research.

Whether they are called scientists, engineers, technologists or
technicians, your technical employees will be responsible for the
conversion of an idea into a tangible product through the application
of known technologies. But, as I found out in my first job in product
development at EG&G in Salem, Massachusetts, this is not as
easy as the words "known technologies" may seem to suggest.

EG&G came to public attention in 1999 when it acquired
the analytical instruments division of Perkin-Elmer in a half-billion
dollar transaction. Less well known is the fact that EG&G's

technology was used by the Manhattan Project and at one time, and perhaps to the present day, EG&G managed the US government's notorious Area 51. This is the secret government test facility that conspiracy theorists credit with being the current home of the UFO that supposedly crashed outside of Roswell, New Mexico, in 1947. For most of its history, EG&G has had a close relationship with government and has been privy to many of the country's most sensitive military secrets. When Eisenhower warned of the growing threat of the military industrial complex, Ike had companies like EG&G in mind.

EG&G grew out of a partnership in the 1930s between Dr. Harold E. Edgerton and two of his former students at the Massachusetts Institute of Technology. Dr. Edgerton spent most of his life in close association with MIT, beginning with his enrollment as a graduate student in 1926 and ending on January 4, 1990, when he succumbed to a heart attack during lunch at the MIT faculty club. Dr. Edgerton had an enthusiasm for one particular subject and the good sense to build his professional life around this singular passion. He loved photography, especially the photography of events impossible for the human eye to perceive. He received the US National Medal of Science in part for his scientific contributions to photography and in part for his practical work in the field. His collaboration with the oceanographer Jacques Cousteau on the research vessel *Calypso* pushed the boundaries of science. In March 1958, National Geographic Magazine credited the two men with exploring "depths far greater than any yet plumbed by photographic man."

For his many technical developments, including the invention of the stroboscope, he was inducted into the National Inventors Hall of Fame. But he also had one invention that was a commercial failure. Camera manufacturers had no interest in licensing his high-speed electronic flash system, but popular culture has provided Dr. Edgerton the last laugh. While the domestic camera industry has faded into obscurity, thanks to the invention they wouldn't buy, the good doctor is more visible than ever. In the summer of 2001, I was in Los Angeles on a road show with an investment banker by the name of Cam Goodnough. When a scheduled full-day presentation at International Rectifier was cut short in the early afternoon, we took advantage of the unexpected break to spend some time with my actor/waiter/student son who lived in the area. Cam and I met Lawrence at a restaurant on Venice Beach. After lunch, the three of us walked along the quirky beach strip with its tattoo artists, fast-food restaurants, massage therapists, street people, tourists from Iowa and hundreds of shops. There, propped against the wall of one of the stalls, was a photograph of a speeding bullet passing through a playing card. Somehow, a magician of photography had caught an event of impossibly short duration on film. It was a miracle of science on display cheek-by-jowl with fortune-tellers and lost souls of every description. The owner of the stall said it was a popular item, a good seller. It was one of Dr. Edgerton's photographs.

During World War II, Dr. Edgerton worked as a technical representative with the US Army Air Force where he applied his expert knowledge of photography to aerial reconnaissance. For his innovative work he later received the Medal of Freedom. More importantly, from the commercial point of view, Dr. Edgerton forged the relationships with the military that resulted in EG&G becoming a prime government contractor. The Atomic Energy Commission needed a manufacturer for certain electronic components, similar to those used in high-speed flash photography, to accurately trigger the detonation of atomic bombs. Early atomic bombs consisted of a mass of fissile material, such as enriched Uranium, surrounded by carefully positioned high-energy explosive charges. When the charges are detonated at precisely the same instant, the fissile material is symmetrically compressed into smaller and smaller volumes until it reaches critical mass, at which time a violent atomic chain reaction ensues. It's a matter of timing that can be provided by the same technology that triggers a flash lamp with the precision necessary to catch a speeding bullet in flight.

My job at EG&G involved testing electron tubes called Krytrons that function as high-speed triggering devices. In size, shape and general appearance, Krytrons look similar to the receiving tubes used in old radio sets. But in performance, Krytrons are very specialized devices used to switch up to thousands of amps and thousands of volts in a very short period of time. The switching is accomplished in an arc-discharge mode, something like a stroke of lightning contained within a glass envelope. Normally, it takes a relatively long period of time for an arc-discharge to occur. In the case of lightning, just prior to the strike an ionized conduction path has been established through a complex and little-understood confluence of physics and chemistry. In the atmosphere, lightning strikes are impossible to predict. But within the confines of a Krytron, an ionized conduction path is "primed" and kept alive by the presence of a small amount of the radioactive isotope Nickel-63. In a sense, the Krytron is designed to create predictable strikes of lightning.

The job of product development was to find the most efficient design that blocked the transmission of high voltage and current until the tube was triggered by an electrical signal. A precise number of nanoseconds after receiving a suitable trigger signal, high voltage and high current were supposed to surge through the tube. You would think complicated physics and mathematical computation would underlie the design of advanced nuclear trigger devices, but the product development process was little more than trial and error. What we did was experiment with the shapes of elements within the trigger tube. There were experiments with rectangular shapes, circular shapes, triangular shapes, oval shapes, shapes pierced with holes and shapes pierced with other shapes. For each of these many shapes, there were additional experiments with various dimensional ratios. The experiments were never-ending, beginning long before my arrival at EG&G and, as far as I know, continuing to this very day.

My experience at EG&G is typical of product development at most companies. The process is rather unscientific, frequently boring, includes more than its fair share of trial and error, and, most importantly and the point of this digression, product development is unpredictable. While certain elements of the process can be placed on a time line, there will be critical factors that cannot be scheduled. For example, it is reasonable to insist that a circuit board be manufactured in a specified period of time. The time to complete such a task is a function of the resources applied to the job. If the task falls behind schedule, you know exactly what needs to be done to bring it back on schedule. All that is needed is the assignment of additional people. On the other hand, it is unreasonable to insist that the circuit board meets its performance specifications by a particular date. There is no sure solution to the problem of completing this kind of task within a specified period of time because no one knows for certain what needs to be done. It's the sort of problem that cannot be resolved by throwing bodies at it. In fact, assigning additional personnel can have an effect opposite to that desired. A popular maxim of the software industry, "A project that three programmers can complete in three weeks can be completed in six weeks by six programmers," speaks directly to this issue.

Management, of course, needs to plan its activities according to a schedule that includes the introduction of new products. Your job is to distinguish between what is and is not technically risky before setting a time line for product development activities. Tasks that are inherently risky need to be flagged. No amount of management bluster can make the risks go away; but through high-level oversight and encouragement, the risks can be managed. Only then is it possible to forecast sales of a future product with a reasonable degree of accuracy, and to make reasonable demands of your product development staff. Insist routine tasks are completed on schedule but, at the same time, acknowledge your personal share of responsibility for completion of the project as a whole. After all, it was you who set the goals.

There is only one reason to undertake the difficult and sometimes unmanageable process of product development. It is to increase sales and to make the company even more profitable. With a sales channel in place that efficiently delivers products to a defined set of customers, one way to sell more is to sell more products to each customer. It's easier to sell two products to one customer than one product to two customers. What's more, the costs of channel development and maintenance are independent of the number of products. As a company increases its line of products, all of which are targeted to the same customer base, the increased efficiency drops to the bottom line as an increase in profitability.

CHAPTER TEN

RTOs and Angels

"An alliance with a powerful person is never safe."
Phaedrus

At some point, you may receive a solicitation from a financial intermediary with an answer to all your present and future financing requirements. There are hundreds of financial intermediaries with telemarketing departments that regularly canvass the entrepreneurial world in the search of clients. However good the story may sound, don't believe it, especially if the financial intermediary demands an up-front payment in return for their services. Typically, the proposal involves either a private placement financing with "the venture capital community and high net worth individuals" or an RTO, a Reverse Take Over of a public company shell.

A private placement financing managed by an opportunistic financial intermediary is usually the kiss of death for an early stage technology company. If the financing does not close, the fact that your company has been unsuccessfully "shopped" will make it extremely difficult to secure other sources of financing. If the financing is successful, the terms usually provide the new investors with effective, if not actual, voting control of the company.

The second alternative, the Reverse Take Over of a public company shell, promises the immediate transformation of the private company into a public company. Public company shells are one-time real operating companies that have failed. These companies, while no longer operational, continue to make the required statutory filings and therefore continue to exist in the legal sense. The public company shell is controlled by a close-knit group of investors who bought their stock for pennies per share. The purpose for acquiring control of a public company shell is to vend it into an operating company, establish a new price and market for the shares, then sell out and make a fortune.

The process to convert a privately owned company with little money and zero liquidity, into a public company with more money and some liquidity, sounds complicated but has been reduced to an art form by its practitioners. The public company shell purchases all the shares of the operating private company from the shareholders of the private company. The public company shell pays for the transaction with new shares it issues from treasury therefore the private company becomes a wholly owned subsidiary of the public company shell. The number of shares issued by the public company shell is more than the number outstanding prior to the transaction; therefore the original shareholders of the private company become the majority shareholders of the public company shell. The subsidiary is merged into its parent and the entity changes its name to one similar to the name of the private company. In effect, the private company has been converted into a public company. Nothing has changed except for its public company status and the additional shareholders. The "new" public company raises capital in the public equity market through a public share offering managed by the financial intermediary. What makes this process especially appealing to the entrepreneur is, thanks to the magic dispensed by a competent lawyer, these seemingly complicated and time consuming steps occur at the same instant in time. There is nothing more seductive than the prospect of immediate gratification.

In my experience, companies that arrange early stage financing through the vehicle of a Reverse Take Over put themselves in a dangerous situation. Usually the amount of money raised in this sort of transaction is only enough to finance operations for a year or so. However, since the company must now look primarily to the public markets for its capital requirements, its ability to complete future financings will depend almost entirely on its stock market performance. But as a micro-cap company, institutions won't buy your stock and analysts won't provide research coverage. These companies are called "orphans" because they are unable to sustain the interest of the public markets. It's a very difficult financial situation. Few orphan companies survive for very long.

The least threatening source of expansion capital comes from a group of wealthy individuals almost too good to be, appropriately named angel investors. Unlike traditional venture capitalists, angel investors are not entirely driven by the profit motive but also by deep-rooted personal beliefs. These individuals, with their business experiences, deep pockets, contacts and supportive attitudes, bring everything to the table an entrepreneur needs and desires. Unfortunately, there are very few true angel investors left. In the eighties and nineties, practically all good-hearted retired business executives were recycled into the role of angel investors. They were the first in and they were the first to lose a bundle. Today, most people who purport to be angel investors are merely shrewd businesspeople.

Finding an angel investor has more to do with being in the right place at the right time than any factor under your control. The last place to find one is at a so-called angel investor conference. Real angel investors do not publicize their existence because they are not primarily interested in making investments. However, if you are in the right place at the right time, and you happen to stumble across a member of this vanishing bread, consider it your lucky day. For the rest of us, there are the venture capitalists. However, before entering their enchanted realm, it's important to understand what you are getting into.

CHAPTER ELEVEN

A History of Venture Capital

"You trust your mama but you cut the cards."
Texas proverb, quoted by Dan Rather

If stereotypes are true, a typical venture capitalist has completed an MBA near the top of his or her class, is outwardly aggressive, thirty-something, and belongs to one of two schools. Members of the Eastern school drive large expensive cars, go skiing in Vermont, wear fashionable clothes, collect modern art, know something about single malt scotch, hate the movies and read the business section first. Members of the Western school drive small expensive cars, go trekking in Nepal, wear casual clothes, collect memorabilia, know something about wine, love the movies and read the sports section first. Members of both schools collect frequent flyer miles and have surprisingly little experience running companies. But don't believe it. Venture capitalists are in many ways like entrepreneurs. They comprise a quirky breed from a variety of backgrounds and are usually knowledgeable about business, sometimes assertive, occasionally trendy but more often traditional, and certainly intelligent. They have more than their fair share of detractors because, in the course of their chosen profession, they reject the great majority of proposals that cross their desks.

The first venture capitalists were self-assured individualists who made investments based on an old-fashioned concept: belief in people. In 1957, when a group of eight scientists became unhappy in their jobs and left their Nobel Prize-winning boss, William Shockley, they were labelled the "traitorous eight." They wanted to form a new kind of company to bring semiconductors out of the laboratory and into the commercial world. Unfortunately, the eight men had little money so they hired a financial consultant named Arthur Rock to find them some. Rock, impressed with the business vision and scientific competence of the group, searched far and wide for the needed capital and in the process was turned down more than thirty times. The conservative financial institutions of the mid-fifties had little interest in technology companies. But Rock persevered and eventually found a wealthy inventor, Sherman Fairchild, who agreed to put up the needed cash and sealed the terms of the deal with a simple handshake.

Fairchild Semiconductor was founded in 1957 and the following year Robert Noyce, one of the traitorous eight, co-invented the integrated circuit. Over the next ten years, Fairchild Semiconductor specialized in the manufacture of a new type of semiconductor device, the linear integrated circuit, and grew into one of the largest technology companies in the world. At about this time, in spite of the success of the company he had helped found, Robert Noyce became frustrated with the direction of Fairchild Semiconductor. Noyce believed the next great opportunity would be in the field of digital integrated circuits, specifically semiconductor memories. Unable to find internal support, Robert Noyce and Gordon Moore, another member of the traitorous eight, left Fairchild Semiconductor and once again sought out Arthur Rock for financial assistance. The two men explained their ideas about practical semiconductor memories that would change the world. Again, Rock was a believer and was successful in raising the financing Robert Noyce and Gordon Moore needed to start Intel Corporation.

Arthur Rock is credited with coining the term "venture capitalist," but bragging rights for inventing the activity itself belong to Rock's professor at the Harvard Business School, General George Doriot. The first company to make what we now refer to as venture capital investments, American Research and Development, was founded in 1946 by Doriot and the then-president of the Federal Reserve Bank in Boston, Ralph Flanders. American Research and Development also scored the first "home run" of the fledgling industry when in 1957 it invested $70,000 for 70% stake in a startup called Digital Equipment Corporation.

The term "venture capitalist" had such powerful resonance that a second wave of technology investors embraced it in self-description. However, unlike General Doriot, these people were not academics, and unlike Arthur Rock, they were not primarily financial specialists. The second wave of venture capitalists consisted of business people. To these experienced individuals, the most important factor in the investment decision was opportunity. Based on experience, they had the ability to look deeply into the character of an entrepreneur and the details of a business, and the self-confidence to make investment decisions based on their personal evaluation. Most of today's venture capital companies were founded, and continue to be led, by members of the second wave.

Ben Webster is an example of a second wave venture capitalist. Ben began his career by introducing the European invention Velcro®® to North America. His company was successful, but after a few years its founder no longer appreciated the allure of the hook-and-loop-fabric business. Ben had a deep-seated understanding of business, but he did not enjoy operations. To be happy, Ben needed involvement in diverse pursuits and, luckily for him, he had the financial resources to supply his own happiness. To make his dream come true, he founded Helix Investments in the late sixties, and over the next thirty years until his death in 1997, Ben's venture capital company helped make dreams come true for entrepreneurs.

For the most part, Ben invested in early stage technology companies when the risk was highest. But, with his keen sense about entrepreneurs and their companies, his investment decisions, in dollar terms, proved to be right more often than otherwise. A few of his early stage investments, for example Geac, Hummingbird, Mitel and Open Text, did remarkably well. However, the most exceptional aspect of the man was not his financial success but his incredible diversity of interests. As a lover of dangerous sports such as bobsledding, Ben invested in a sporting equipment company. As a lover of the mysteries of the past, Ben invested in a treasure hunt. As a lover of the occult, Ben financed over one million experiments at Princeton University to demonstrate the power of the human mind to control electrical and mechanical phenomena at distances up to several thousand miles. Every successful venture capitalist is able to make a connection with the entrepreneurs they sponsor. Arthur Rock connected with entrepreneurs he believed in and General Doriot connected with entrepreneurs he understood. In Ben's case, he connected with entrepreneurs who shared a mutual interest in history, sports, or the occult. His offices, occupying the top floor of an office building, showcased an eclectic collection of antiquities, furniture and art. The eighteenth century boardroom table was made of fine West Indian reddish brown mahogany. Upon the numerous sideboards, relics of Hindu maharajas were displayed alongside examples of the latest technical gismos, and a magnificent Victorian oil painting of the Sphinx kept guard over the central hallway.

Ben was a hard-nosed experienced businessman who knew how to have fun. When an acquaintance opened a business in the Soviet Union, Ben purchased a life-sized statue of Lenin and had it permanently installed in man's backyard. On another occasion, after a particularly good year, Ben flew his entrepreneurs to Saint Moritz where there was skiing to exercise the body and, to inspire the spirit, a presentation by the psychic Uri Geller of the spoon-bending power of the mind. Fun loving and serious at the same time, Ben made quick decisions and, like Arthur Rock, sealed them with a handshake, or even less. When CRS Robotics Corporation needed a loan of $1 million on short order, the deal was made in a ten-minute telephone call and the check arrived the next day. In typical Ben Webster fashion, it was hand-written.

Beginning in the mid 1980s and fueled by the explosive growth of the software industry, venture capital embarked on its greatest period of growth. To meet demand, venture capital firms began to hire graduates directly out of business school. This third wave of venture capitalists had neither the life experience to believe in people nor the business experience to believe in companies. All they believed in were the numbers and they worked them diligently. There were hockey-stick projections, off balance sheet financings, and valuations based entirely on future performance. They financed everything from e-business companies selling immediate access to sacks of dog food, to biotechnology companies with an idea for a billion dollar drug. The third wave of venture capitalists contributed more than their fair share, in my opinion, to that great speculative bubble that grew for more than a decade then burst in an orgy of insider trading and fraud.

In recent years, as has been the case with many of the companies they sponsor, venture capital firms have downsized. The ranks of the third wave have been thinned. The surviving members are generally competent but most of them continue to suffer, in my opinion, from an excessively analytical view of the world. They will understand the numbers, and your numbers are pretty good, but many of them will not appreciate your verbal presentation, your body language, or your enthusiasm. Yet all is not lost. The senior partners at most venture capital firms have the business experience needed to value your company beyond the numbers, based on an appreciation of your personal ability, the accomplishments to date and the market opportunity. It is to these salty dogs that you should direct your appeal.

CHAPTER TWELVE

Preparing for Venture Capital

"As I grow older, I pay less attention to what people say.
I just watch what they do."
Andrew Carnegie

Most Business Plans turned down by venture capitalists, for reasons other than the Business Plan itself, are rejected because "suitable management is not in place." This polite euphemism refers to the fact that the entrepreneur who has brought the proposal to the table will not, in the opinion of the venture capitalist, make a suitable Chief Executive Officer. Usually the offending defect is neither of character nor experience, but simply the inability to communicate the opportunity in acceptable financial terminology. Few entrepreneurs are trained in accounting, yet Chief Executive Officers of companies backed by venture capitalists are expected to have a reasonable understanding of the subject.

The amount of detail contained in the Seed Round Financial Forecast sufficient for the seed round investors, but is far less than what a venture capitalist will require. They will expect to receive financial information in a standard format. If you do not already know something about the subject, you will need to acquire some knowledge about accounting and Financial Statements before presenting your company to a venture capitalist. Even if you have a Chief Financial Officer who is responsible for compilations, you still need a basic understanding of the subject. It is absolutely essential that you can explain your business strategies in terms of Financial Statement impact.

I recommend you compile your company's financial information in a spreadsheet document called the Operational Plan. The Operational Plan contains all the detail that would be found in a company's Financial Statements, but in a more practical format. The purpose of Financial Statements is to record the company's performance during a past period of time, for example the year ending December 31, 2002, or the third quarter of the year ending September 30, 2003. In contrast, the Operational Plan also includes a forecast. The Appendix contains a complete explanation of the Operational Plan and its preparation.

The Operational Plan gives the entrepreneur the ability to ask "what if" questions because assumptions plugged into the document recalculate the spreadsheet, and the potential impact on every line item in the forecasted Financial Statements can be immediately appreciated. The Operational Plan is the entrepreneur's best tool for managing risk while developing and executing effective strategies, and will be considered a sign of good management by a venture capitalist. However, a venture capitalist will want to evaluate the Operational Plan within the larger context of a written Business Plan. To write it most efficiently, build the Operational Plan first. It's easier to write the text after the numbers have been crunched. Once the numbers are in hand, start writing the Business Plan with the second section. The first section, the management summary, should be written after you have completed the rest of the document and have something to summarize.

The second section describes business model and growth strategy. The reason you are seeking an investment is to finance growth. Explain how fast the company is growing and how, in the interests of prudent business management, it has been necessary to turn away business. What the venture capitalist wants to hear is that the new money will be used to satisfy customer demand, not to create customer demand. Venture capitalists do not want to pay for expensive marketing campaigns. If you plan to expand the sales organization, explain that new employees will be hired after sales have reached a certain level, not in order to grow sales to a certain level. Describe the company's sales channels and explain why they are appropriate for its products and customers. The business model of the company is to manufacture its products and take them to market in the most efficient and most profitable manner possible. In particular, venture capitalists want to make sure you know the importance of leverage because an entrepreneur who wants to build an empire is of no interest to them. Tell them your company will manufacture only what it must manufacture, and anything that should be outsourced will be outsourced.

The next topic is market. Define the market in terms of your customers. Your company is not part of the market; it sells into the market. Make your case that the market is sizable and rapidly growing. Include charts estimating the size of the market from two different sets of input data: "top down" based on the historical sales of competitors, and "bottom up" based on the historical consumption of customers. Extrapolate the historical trend lines to establish the market is expanding and use the Sales Pipeline to illustrate that the company is well positioned to participate in the growth. Include a description of current customers with details of their historical and projected requirement for your products.

The fourth section outlines the competitive environment. This section is usually placed somewhere near the back of the document. That's a mistake. What the venture capitalist really wants to know is the potential value of your company, and there is no better benchmark for this than the value of your competitors. Include a table with the market capitalization (number of shares times price per share) of public companies that sell into your market. Financial analysts call these data sets "comparables" in the belief that the value of public company competitors is a good indicator of a private company's future value. Make liberal use of the concept.

The fifth section is about products. Describe products in terms of the commercial advantage conveyed to your customers. Don't dwell on technical matters; rather explain why your customers will need to purchase your products due to their unique features such as size, weight, speed, or technical specifications. Unique features make a compelling case, but a low price strategy is a flawed strategy. Even if your manufacturing costs are much lower than the competition, it is better to sell on the basis of unique features and set competitive, not lower, prices. Explain that you have been and will continue to make high profits, and are steadily building the business.

Do not include a section on research and development. In fact, avoid the use of the phrase "research and development" because it implies that the investment will involve a technology development risk. Future products will be based on the intellectual property that has already been developed and patented, and need only to be run through a proven design and development process.

Having described your products, establish the fact that you own them. The sixth section is about intellectual property. List and briefly describe the company's patents and other intellectual property. Explain how the unique features of your product, those that convey a commercial advantage to your customers and enable the product to be sold at high margins, are the exclusive monopoly of your company due to its ownership of intellectual property.

The seventh and final section is for financial information. Include copies of previous annual Financial Statements and the Operational Plan. If the Operational Plan includes an estimate of venture round proceeds, remember to delete it. It's perfectly acceptable to show a negative cash balance in future periods.

Having described your business opportunity in considerable detail in sections two through seven, it's time to describe the opportunity in as little detail as possible. The purpose of the management summary is to get the attention of the reader and it must ring with focus. Your company is fast growing and has more business than it can handle. The appropriateness of the business model and management's ability to execute has been demonstrated by past performance. The company is selling a product at high margins. The high margins are a consequence of the cost structure enabled by the company's patented intellectual property. The market for your product is rapidly growing and the success of the company is not dependent on taking market share away from anybody. Point out the unique features of one specific product. Avoid technical details. In purely commercial terms, describe how the unique features of the product are important to and have resulted in orders from your best well-known customer. Finally, do not mention the amount of investment being sought.

After you have finished the first draft of the Business Plan, if it seems thin bulk it up with additional material. Illustrations, a section of management biographies, and a general discussion of manufacturing, quality and facilities can be added to the document without detracting from its focus. A finished document about a half-inch thick is a nice size.

CHAPTER THIRTEEN

Obtaining Venture Capital

"Nothing will ever be attempted,
if all possible objections must first be overcome."
Samuel Johnson

Venture capital firms spend a majority of their time working with their portfolio companies and a minority of their time looking for new places to invest. But even if venture capitalists were to spend all of their time evaluating new opportunities, they would come up short. There are simply too many people looking for money and never enough time. Venture capitalists are very much like window shoppers. It is difficult to get their attention, and even more difficult to make the sale.

Most of the money invested by venture capital firms is not their own. It comes from institutional investors such as mutual funds, life insurance companies, banks and pension funds. The fierce competition for institutional money, and the fact that people make better decisions about subjects they understand, has resulted in most venture capital firms becoming quite specialized. The fields of specialization can be quite narrow, for example financial software companies in the Northeast. It is therefore very important to understand what opportunities would be of interest to a particular venture capital firm before making an approach. Luckily, there is a substantial amount of information about venture capital firms available on the Internet. In an afternoon, you should be able to compile a list of appropriate firms, the names of their senior partners, and the companies in which they have invested including the names of the Chief Executive Officers. Incidentally, if a firm has an investment in a direct competitor, drop it from you list. In a competitive situation, venture capitalists usually bet on one horse at a time.

Now the hard part begins. While entrepreneurs must track down every possible lead in search of customers, venture capitalists operate in a completely different environment. Their task is not to find customers, but to sort through them. Like book publishers, venture capitalists want to see the manuscript before talking to the author. From your point of view, this is definitely the wrong sequence of events. Your goal is to personally explain the opportunity before handing over the Business Plan. You want to start with a face-to-face meeting with a senior partner.

Arranging such meetings begins with telephone calls and, before senior partners in venture capital firms will take your calls, you need referrals. If you already know the right people, the task at hand will be considerably simplified. If not, the best strategy to gain access to the senior partners is through the Chief Executive Officers in their portfolio. Make a list of your acquaintances that might be in a position to help including lawyers, accountants, consultants, recruiters, but especially people who run companies, and start telephoning. Explain what you are doing and ask for referrals to the chief executives. In any community, business people know business people and every chief executive on your list probably has a business relationship with at least one person you know. Before long, you will have a referral to a chief executive who can connect you with a senior partner at each of the venture capital firms. At this point, it is important to understand a little more about the expectations of a venture capitalist before actually speaking to one.

The venture capitalist wants to make money. Since this is accomplished by putting money into your company, and the venture capitalist's profit will depend on how much money is invested and upon what terms, entrepreneurs tend to bring up the issue of valuation during the first meeting. That's a big mistake. Venture capitalists do not want to discuss valuation. They want to understand the business of the company. In the process of coming to that understanding, the venture capitalist will determine what she or he thinks the company needs to accomplish and the smallest amount of money that will be required. After the smallest possible amount of money has been determined, then and only then is the venture capitalist ready to talk valuation.

Valuation can wait for later because the venture capitalist expects to own a certain percentage of the company, usually 40% in the case of an early stage technology company, regardless the amount of the investment. In other words, the valuation will be a function of the amount invested and, as surely as the sun goes down over Santa Monica Boulevard, the investment will be no more, and usually less, than the amount the company needs. I say "usually less" because the venture capitalist has a vested interest to put in less money than the needed amount. The venture capitalist wants the money to run out. If the company is a loser when the money runs out, the venture capital firm has effectively cut its losses. If the company is a winner when the money runs out, the venture capitalist can be a hero and step in with a bridge loan to tide the company over until additional financing is arranged. Of course, even heroes expect to be compensated for their efforts, and the bridge loan will have provisions that provide an additional upside. Venture capitalists love upside. This reasoning may seem a little devious but such considerations are hard-wired into the venture capital brain.

Therefore, if the venture capital firm wants to own 40% of the company after the financing is completed, and the amount of money to be invested is no more than the smallest amount needed, the *maximum* pre-money valuation for the venture round is 150% of the *smallest* amount needed by the company. For example, if the venture capital firm thinks the company will need $1 million to take it to the next stage, it will want to invest no more than $1 million. In order for $1 million to buy 40% of the shares, the pre-money valuation is 150% of $1 million, or $1.5 million, and the post-money valuation is therefore $2.5 million. To double-check the math, 40% of $2.5 million is $1 million. It doesn't seem fair, but the valuation of your company has more to do with the amount of money you need than with the past performance and future potential of your business.

Venture capitalists will tell you they want companies with focus, a large and growing market, and high margins protected by intellectual property. But this is not literally true. These commendable qualities are but a means to an end. What they want is a return on their investment, a high return. A venture capitalist might be quoted in a business magazine professing their firm's goal is to achieve an annualized return of 30%, but he or she is being truthful only in an average sense. Since most venture capital investments bear no return at all, the winners must return considerably more than average. Venture capitalists need big winners and they look for big winners.

Venture capital firms also need liquidity. For the most part, venture capital firms manage large pools of capital that are contributed by institutional investors and exist within a legal entity called a limited partnership. Each pool of capital is called a fund, and each fund has specific investment objectives including liquidity. In this regard, most venture capital funds are created to operate for a period of seven to ten years and, even more to the point, the venture capital firm does not participate in the profits (its cut is about 20%) until after the full amount contributed by the limited partners has been repaid. Obviously, no venture capital firm will make an investment unless there is a likelihood of liquidity within the available time frame.

At this point, with your list of chief executives and a somewhat jaded opinion of the venture capital exercise, once again it's time to make telephone calls. Chief Executive Officers are easy to make contact with if you happen to be a member of their species. Tell the assistant who answers the phone, "I'm the Chief Executive Officer of New Products Corporation and I need to talk to Bob." You will either be put through or your call will be returned. In an easy, conversational tone, mention you were referred by a mutual friend. Tell your fellow chief executive a little bit about you and your company. Elicit a response. Chances are the person at the other end of the line will also have something to say. After you have established a rapport, explain your reason for calling. But don't ask to use their name, ask them to use their name. Ask them to telephone the senior partner of the venture capital firm and request that he or she take your call. Making such a request of a total stranger requires a certain amount of *chutzpah* but it's also a good indicator of whether or not you have what it takes, something better to know sooner rather than later.

The senior partner at the venture capital firm will be expecting your call, so he or she will probably take it or phone you back. When you do make contact, your goal is to get a face-to-face meeting. The danger to avoid is the request to forward your Business Plan before the face-to-face meeting. The best way to steer clear of this disaster is to pre-empt it. In an unstressed conversational tone, in about sixty seconds describe your company, its success and your experience. When you have finished, wait for a response. Try to foster a conversation, but at the first sign that the discussion is waning, end the conversation with a request. "I have a lunch on Wednesday near your office. Can I drop off a copy of the Business Plan before noon or after two?" If there is any hesitation at all, continue with, "Or, I can pop in at the end of the day. Will you be available then?" Now, after engaging in polite conversation and making two attempts to schedule a meeting, you have the psychological high ground. The dreaded, "I want to have a look at your Business Plan first," would now be borderline rude. Your target will probably acquiesce or suggest an alternate date and time. If not, and you receive the dreaded response, counter with, "Fine, I'll deliver it in person. Can you give me the name of an associate I can telephone to set it up?" A meeting with an associate is better than no meeting at all.

When you get your meeting count on several attendees. The usual practice at venture capital firms is to avoid one-on-one meetings early in the process. But, in spite of the additional ears brought to the table, remember venture capitalists are always looking for reasons to stop listening to you and move on to the next supplicant. Don't make chit chat. Distribute copies of the Business Plan but don't open yours and don't encourage them to open theirs. Get immediately down to business. Tell them what they want to hear. In Los Angeles this exercise would be called a "pitch." Tell them your company sells a product with unique features enabled by proprietary and patented intellectual property. Tell them profit margins are high, your cost is low, and you don't compete on price. Tell them the market for your product is rapidly growing, success is not dependent on taking market share away from established competitors, your sales channel is in place, and there is already more business than you can handle. Once more, it is important to make this presentation in a relaxed, conversational tone. Make them feel comfortable enough to interrupt and ask questions. When finished, ask for a description of the firm's usual procedure to evaluate opportunities and listen to the response. Don't take notes. Don't ask for a follow-on meeting, but do table an invitation for the group to visit your company. Your presentation is finished. Thank them for their time. Flash your most confident smile.

It's their turn to make a move. If you don't hear back in a week, you might as well telephone and hear the bad news. But if there is interest, in a few days you will receive a call from an associate "just to fill in a few details." This is the beginning of a process that will involve back and forth telephone calls for about a week, then you will be asked to make another presentation. After the second presentation, which will be similar to the first and followed by many questions now that the audience has read the Business Plan, a delegation from the venture capital firm will visit your facility. After that, there will be at least one meeting with either a member of the venture capital firm or an outside consultant. The purpose of this meeting is to examine the company's technology in minute detail. This process, of course, will be going on with multiple venture capital firms at the same time. Juggling their demands can be a considerable challenge, but the situation is only temporary. Eventually one of them will present a Term Sheet setting out proposed conditions for a financing. The next step is to call a meeting of the Board of Directors. If the terms and conditions are found acceptable, management will be authorized to accept the Term Sheet on behalf of the company.

Issuer:	New Products Corporation
Investor:	KBF Capital Partners
Amount:	$1,000,000
Price per share:	$0.75
Closing date:	(About 30 days)
Securities to be acquired:	1,333,333 Series A Preferred Shares
Capitalization:	Prior to closing, the capitalization of the Company shall consist of 2,500,000 Common Shares.
Rights of Series A Preferred Shares:	(1) The Series A Preferred Shares shall have the right to vote on an equal basis with the Common Shares on all matters.
	(2) The Series A Preferred Shares shall rank in preference to Common Shares with respect to dividends and liquidation.
	(3) The Series A Preferred Shares shall be convertible into Common Shares at any time upon the option of the holders and will be automatically converted upon completion of a Qualified Initial Public Offering (QIPO) with minimum proceeds of $15 million and a minimum price three times the price of this round.
Board of Directors:	The board shall consist of five members consisting of at least one independent member and two members appointed by KBF Capital Partners.
Other conditions:	(1) Satisfactory completion of due diligence.
	(2) The approval of the Investment Committee of KBF Capital Partners.
	(3) KBF Capital Partners, the Company and its shareholders will enter into a shareholders' agreement on terms satisfactory to KBF Capital Partners.
Exclusivity:	The Company will not seek financing from any third party for a period of ninety days.
Expenses:	The Company agrees to reimburse KBF Capital Partners for the legal and accounting expenses of the proposed transaction.
Expiration:	This term sheet will expire unless it is signed and returned by the Company prior to (about one week).

Table 4. Venture Capital Term Sheet

The venture capitalists will already have spoken to your top customers and, judging from the results, your customers provided glowing references in spite of the fact that you have been too busy to pay much attention to them lately. Your focus, during the period from acceptance of the Term Sheet until closing, must be redirected back to your customers. The venture capitalists will likely make a second set of customer calls before closing. In this sort of investment decision, the single most important factor over which you have some measure of control is customer feedback.

Over the coming weeks, a process of "due diligence" will be going on in the background. You will have some involvement but the majority of these activities involve a detailed inspection of corporate and financial records conducted between your lawyer and a law firm acting for the venture capital firm. The lawyers will also spend considerable time drafting a set of agreements that specify the exact details of the investment based on the conditions summarized in the Term Sheet. There will be many documents to sign. Finally, when sufficient undertakings, warranties and indemnities have been received, there will be a formal closing in a law firm boardroom and stacks of paperwork will be exchanged between the lawyers. Almost as an afterthought, an associate lawyer will hand you a file folder containing a big check.

CHAPTER FOURTEEN

Biotechnology

"Any sufficiently advanced technology is indistinguishable from magic."
Arthur C. Clarke

There is a bewildering diversity of biotechnology companies; nevertheless, most belong to one of two groups that have similar business strategy issues and financing requirements. Members of the first group are sometimes called "Platform" companies. These companies have products that are used in the discovery, production or delivery of drugs. The gene chip company Affymetrix, the restriction enzyme company New England Biolabs, and the genomics company Incyte, are Platform companies. In terms of business strategy and financing, there is little difference between a Platform company in the biotechnology industry and a company in the software, semiconductor or other more traditional technology industry. The second group comprises the majority of biotechnology companies. It consists of companies that intentionally plan to have a negative cash flow for many years. Most of these companies are in the drug development business, but any biotechnology company with products that are subject to lengthy regulatory approval processes is a member of this group.

For a traditional technology company, the completion of its venture capital financing round is a notable accomplishment. It has successfully assembled a staff and management team, built an operational infrastructure, and converted its intellectual property into a commercially valuable product that is being manufactured and sold. At the close of the venture capital round, a traditional technology company is no longer a startup. In contrast, in the biotechnology industry the typical company *begins* life with a venture capital investment. Sometimes this first round is called a "seed round," but other than in name, there is no similarity with the process described in Chapter Four. Instead of unsophisticated investors who bring a small amount of money but little else to the table, the participants of this seed round are professional venture capitalists who not only make a sizeable investment but also provide advice, access to industry contacts, and practical help building the business.

Compared to an entrepreneur in a traditional technology company, the founder of a biotechnology company enjoys three impressive advantages. First, there is access to startup capital and professional business development assistance. Second, the role of a biotechnology entrepreneur can be exceptionally challenging and rewarding. For example, instead of the mundane work of sales management there is "business development," an activity primarily concerned with identifying partners and negotiating agreements. The entrepreneur assumes the lead role in these matters and has the opportunity to make full use of his or her business and negotiation skills at a much earlier stage of corporate development than in a traditional technology company. The third advantage is increased ownership. After the venture capital round the founding entrepreneur usually owns less than 50% of a traditional technology company, but more than 50% of a biotechnology company.

So far, this sounds pretty good for biotechnology entrepreneurs, but there is a big downside. They may start out at the head of the pack but by the time of the Initial Public Offering, biotechnology entrepreneurs on average own significantly less of their companies than their counterparts at traditional technology companies. As if this were not bad enough, comparatively fewer venture-backed biotechnology companies make it to the IPO stage and, even worse, the Chief Executive Officer of a biotechnology company at the time of its Initial Public Offering is, more often than not, someone other than the company's founder. The reasons for this distressing state of affairs are ingrained in the business development and financing practices of the biotechnology industry.

Very often, venture capital investments in biotechnology companies are structured differently than investments in traditional technology companies. Instead of receiving the full amount on closing, biotechnology companies may receive installments called tranches that are subject to meeting defined milestones, and if the company does not meet its milestones, the original deal is subject to renegotiation. Whether or not funds are subject to successful completion of formal milestones, however, there is one milestone every biotechnology entrepreneur wants to achieve before the next round of financing. It's called third-party validation. Without it, the next financing round will seriously dilute the entrepreneur's ownership.

The highest level of third-party validation is a partnership deal with one of the dozen or so huge pharmaceutical corporations collectively known as "Big Pharma." Next down the pecking order are about one hundred companies that are much smaller than the eminent few but nevertheless qualify as legitimate pharmaceutical companies. Some of these companies are quite specialized in terms of products or geographical markets served, most are little-known outside the industry, but all possess three essential attributes: they conduct research, they manufacture drugs and they have a sales organization. In a typical partnership deal, the biotechnology company receives payments, subject to achieving defined milestones, and the pharmaceutical company receives an option, usually an exclusive option, to license one or more products. But there's a problem with the numbers. There are too many biotechnology companies, about five thousand, compared to the number of potential pharmaceutical partners. The ratio works out to a fifty-to-one shot, but the actual probability of achieving third-party validation is even less than that because few biotechnology companies begin serious discussions with pharmaceutical companies before the first round of venture capital financing runs out.

The first round of venture capital is usually enough to fund operations for 18 to 24 months, but not much more. Some of this time will be wasted while the new company locates suitable premises and builds out the needed laboratory space. Even if the new company moves into a fully equipped incubator facility, it will take time to hire and train staff, and to prioritize what needs to be done and to begin doing it. After this initial nonproductive period, the first business development initiatives will be taken. More often than not, the entrepreneur delegates the legwork to a newly hired executive who has been recruited from the pharmaceutical industry. This person will need time to get up to speed on the product and the company's proprietary science, and more time to write a business development plan. By the time the company presents its story to a real pharmaceutical company for the first time, it will have less than one year to achieve third-party validation.

Most early-stage biotechnology companies schedule their business development activities around industry events that have been organized for the purpose. The Biotechnology Industry Organization, for example, sponsors conferences in North America, Europe and Asia where biotechnology companies can showcase their products to an audience from the pharmaceutical industry. These venues can be quite useful, but they are also expensive, sometimes nonproductive, and always time consuming. The pharmaceutical companies attend these gatherings to keep abreast of industry developments and to make preliminary contacts with potential partners, but not to seriously negotiate relationship agreements. The best outcome a biotechnology company can hope for is to enter at the bottom of lengthy and bureaucratic process. Eventually, if interest can be sustained through a series of follow-on meetings at six to eight week intervals, there will be a presentation to a decision maker. Then, if the decision maker likes the story, there will either be additional scientific due diligence or the parties will move directly to the final three to six month process of negotiating a business agreement.

More often than not, however, the process never really gets started. The first thing most biotechnology companies learn in their first meeting with a pharmaceutical company is that the meeting is premature. A pre-clinical drug candidate, all the company has at this point in time, is of little value to a pharmaceutical company. The pharmaceutical company will have no interest until safety and efficacy have been demonstrated in animal studies, and the company has filed an Investigative New Drug (IND) application with the Food and Drug Administration (FDA).

Unfortunately, by the time this message has been received and understood, time and money have run out. Usually the founding entrepreneur survives the second round of venture capital financing with his or her job intact, but from this point forward there will be an undercurrent of dissatisfaction and the venture capitalists, the new majority shareholders, will assume a more intrusive role in the affairs of the company. The entrepreneur's actions will be subject to increased scrutiny and, unless business development progress is made prior to the third financing round, usually a change is made at the top. Typically, an experienced business executive is brought in as the new Chief Executive Officer and the founding entrepreneur is moved to the sidelines as Chief Scientific Officer.

The best way for a founding entrepreneur to protect himself, or herself, against this all too common scenario is to preempt it. Build a time cushion into your business plan by raising enough cash in the first venture capital round to fund operations for three years. If this is not possible, scale back your expenses to make the amount received last for three years, and under any circumstances do not agree to unrealistic performance milestones. With the money in the bank, your first priority is to hire an experienced person to begin writing the IND application. At this point, it will not be possible to complete the IND application but the missing pieces will set the operational focus. Your goal is to direct the scientific resources of the company to fill in the blanks, enabling the filing of the document with the FDA at the earliest opportunity.

Building a biotechnology company is inextricably linked to the FDA clinical trial process. The first step, filing an IND application, leads to Phase I clinical trials. These trials demonstrate the safety of the drug in healthy humans. Pharmaceutical companies may begin to show interest when the IND application has been filed, but more typically pharmaceutical companies want the Phase I clinical trials successfully completed before their level of interest becomes serious. Your objective is to complete a Phase I clinical trial before the first round of venture capital financing runs out.

It is never too soon to begin discussions with pharmaceutical companies, even if it is too early for them to be seriously interested in what you have to say. What you want is to get on their radar screen, and to make and develop contacts with decision makers. This preliminary work will significantly shorten the time required to negotiate a future deal. However, before packing your bags for the next pharmaceutical partnership conference, make a list of the companies you want to pursue. Look for companies that are not developing a drug similar to your own and do not have existing partnership agreements with your biotechnology competitors, but do have a suitable sales and marketing channel for your drug.

Not only do pharmaceutical companies have little interest in early-stage drugs, but also the further along your drug is in the developmental pipeline, the more a deal will be worth. It's a win-win situation. The strategy most likely to result in a deal is also the highest value strategy. Approach your targeted list of pharmaceutical companies with a specific proposal: would they be interested in a deal *after* you complete Phase I clinical trials? In effect, a positive response to such a proposal is an agreement to continue discussions and to build a deeper relationship in the interim—exactly what you desire.

With a pharmaceutical company partnering deal beginning at the Phase II clinical trial stage under your belt, a reasonable valuation for the second venture capital round should be a sure thing. The proceeds should be sufficient to fund operations for about two years until the completion of the Phase II clinical trials. The purpose of Phase II clinical trials is to demonstrate safety in patients suffering from the condition the drug is supposed to treat. If these trials are successfully completed, there will be a mezzanine round of financing in which investors outside the venture capital community will participate. The mezzanine round will fund operations until the company and its pharmaceutical partner begin Phase III clinical trials. This is the final stage of the clinical trial process that determines whether or not the drug performs as advertised. Most biotechnology companies complete their Initial Public Offerings shortly after Phase III clinical trials have begun.

CHAPTER FIFTEEN

Liquidity

*"A person usually has two reasons for doing something:
a good reason and the real reason."*
Thomas Carlyle

At New Products Corporation, high growth has been coupled with a steady increase in operational efficiency because high profitability has allowed continual reinvestment in infrastructure. Its operational systems have improved over time. New production processes and better scheduling, training and quality systems, have resulted in a steady decrease in manufacturing costs. Upgraded information technology and communications systems have led to improvements in purchasing, inventory management, accounting, invoicing, collections, customer service and sales. In its fourth year of operations, sales are expected to total about $4 million. Yet, in spite of the success, in the boardroom there is an undercurrent of discontent.

While performance has been undeniably excellent, the satisfaction of the venture capital and seed round investors is tempered by the absence of liquidity. Outside investors want liquidity and the clock is always ticking. The outside investors' dissatisfaction will grow until eventually, because they own a combined 52% of the company, the investors will get their way. Sooner or later, small private companies controlled by outside investors are forced to adopt a business strategy that includes liquidity for the investors. Like puberty in humans, this is a point in the life of a venture-backed technology company that is unavoidable.

There are two mutually exclusive liquidity options available, the first of which is to sell the company and cash out now. In this case, the prospective buyer would be a company large enough to make an acquisition in cash or its equivalent. Such a buyer would want intellectual property, product lines, customers and key technical individuals, but probably not want additional manufacturing and administrative facilities. The sale would provide an ongoing role for the entrepreneur and attractive jobs for key employees but, after a suitable transition period, low-level employees would be out of luck, the production facility would be relocated, and the rest of the physical plant would be broken up and sold. If the price is right, outside investors love the option of selling out, but management usually hates it whatever the price.

The other option is to cash out later, and there are two potential strategies leading to its accomplishment for the Board of Directors to ponder. The first is to grow the company quickly to position it for an Initial Public Offering, but there are a number of difficulties that make this strategy, one that worked so well during the eighties and nineties, impractical. Companies are no longer taken public on the basis of potential alone. Today, it is necessary for the potential to be proven by a track record that includes reaching a minimum size of about $20 million in sales. Starting from a revenue base of $4 million at the end of the current year, achieving such a level will probably take three to six years. Management loves the IPO option because it validates their accomplishments and empowers them to continue, but outside investors may be lukewarm the idea. They want liquidity sooner than in three to six years, and would also prefer to have more liquidity than that provided by shares in a very small public company.

However, there is a second strategy in pursuit of the second option that may be acceptable to all. It is to build the company into a much larger entity through acquisitions and consolidations and, once that larger size has been attained, to either merge it into an established public company where it will live on as a separate operating division, or take it public. This strategy is acceptable to both seed round investors and management, and it is more than acceptable to a venture capital firm. It is, in fact, the favorite strategy pursued by venture capital firms at the present time (2003) to "work out" their portfolios through the consolidation of smaller companies into larger companies. The venture capital firm can rely on management at the healthier company, for example a company such as New Products Corporation or your company, to support a consolidation that places a larger business under their operational control.

As an alternative to adding size through consolidation of a venture capital portfolio, there is also the possibility of taking the business to the next level through the acquisition of a competitor. In early 1995 for example, CRS Robotics Corporation was a profitable and growing company only half as large as needed to complete an Initial Public Offering. Our strategy to overcome the size issue was to acquire a competitor in Germany. The two companies were an excellent fit because their products were compatible, they served geographically separate markets, each company had exclusive products that the other company could sell to existing customers, and the owners of the German company had the same liquidity issues as the investors in CRS. We made a down payment of $1 million (borrowed from Ben Webster at Helix) and completed the transaction a few months later with a portion of the proceeds from the Initial Public Offering.

Whether a company markedly increases its size to a liquidity point through growth, consolidation, acquisition, or a combination of strategies, there will likely be costs that cannot be financed out of cash flow and it will become necessary to secure additional working capital. Your venture capital partner will point out that the company will be worth more after it has attained size and therefore it would be preferable to postpone raising capital until a higher valuation can be achieved. Also, a financing at this point in time is counterproductive because management would lose its focus on operations during a critical period of growth. As a solution, the venture capital firm will offer to provide a bridge loan that will be converted into equity on the same terms and conditions as the next round of financing. This continued commitment of venture capital is exactly what new investors will want to see, the self-justification will conclude.

The full terms of the bridge loan will be spelled out in a Term Sheet. The interest rate will be 5-10% above prime. That may seem high, but it's a fairly typical rate for bridge loans because of the level of risk. Usually business loans are secured against specific assets, for example accounts receivable, that limit the risk to the lender and keeps the interest rate down. But a bridge loan, called subordinated debt in the financial community, is not backed up by a specific asset and is therefore riskier. In addition to the high interest rate there will be some form of "sweetener," usually a warrant, attached to the transaction. A warrant entitles the holder to purchase Common Shares in the company at a predetermined price per share, usually the price of the most recently completed financing round. Dividing the amount of the loan by the exercise price per share and multiplying this result by a percentage called the warrant coverage, determines the number of shares that a warrant entitles its holder to purchase. The amount of coverage ranges between 25 to 100 percent, depending on the avarice of the venture capitalist and the negotiating skills of the company's Chief Executive Officer. The warrant is valid for a specified term, usually two or three years, during which time it can be exercised at the option of the holder, except in the event of a Qualified Initial Public Offering in which case the warrant expires unless exercised. For example, in the case of New Products Corporation, 50% warrant coverage on a $1 million bridge loan obligates the company to issue 666,667 warrants exercisable at $0.75 per Common Share.

CHAPTER SIXTEEN

Stock Options

"Better to be nouveau than never to be riche at all."
Anonymous

As the company begins to implement its new business strategy that includes liquidity for the investors, there will be changes to the Board of Directors. Independent directors, with contacts and experiences that will help the company address the issues it now faces, will be added to the Board, and an experienced corporate secretary, who may or may not be a member of the Board, will be appointed. The secretary has a number of specific duties in law, such as signing certain documents on behalf of the company, but his or her responsibility is to document Board activity for inclusion in the company's minute book. Since the state of completeness of the minute book can become an issue at the most inopportune times, for example during the Initial Public Offering, the position is frequently filled by a corporate lawyer. In return for this service, and also for the services of the independent directors, the usual practice for technology companies at this stage of development is to issue Stock Options in lieu of cash compensation.

The restructured Board of Directors will conduct its affairs in a more formal manner than in the past. Each year, there will be four regularly scheduled meetings, with each meeting approximately five weeks after the end of a fiscal quarter. In an increasing number of smaller companies that wish to adopt the best practices of corporate governance, an audit committee chaired by and composed of a majority of independent directors, will review quarterly Financial Statements and formally recommend the acceptance, or the alternative, to the Board. In addition, a compensation committee will be similarly composed to make formal recommendations to the Board about executive remuneration and Stock Options. I think it is a good practice to keep directors informed of the company's activities by routinely sending copies of company materials such as data sheets, advertisements and newspaper articles. In addition, it's a good idea to include directors on the distribution list for WAR Reports. It is theoretically possible to give directors more information than needed, but that's one complaint I've never heard.

One of the first actions of the new Board will be to pass an Employee Stock Option Plan, an ESOP, to formalize the process of awarding Stock Options to new and existing employees. The plan will set out the provisions of the company's Stock Options including vesting, exercise, expiry, and rights upon termination or death. Your lawyer will have such a plan in boilerplate format and will be able to run one off to meet the specific requirements of your company in short order. A reasonable level of Stock Option compensation for each year of service by an independent director or corporate secretary is $10,000 in options. This number is the amount paid per share at the company's most recent financing divided into $10,000, rounded up to the next hundred.

Stock Options are a valuable tool for a technology company on the verge of significant growth. Through judicious use of Stock Options, the company can recruit key employees whom might otherwise be too expensive or are reluctant to change jobs. For other members of your work force, Stock Options are a valuable incentive that helps keep employee turnover to a minimum. The maximum number of Stock Options issued is usually about 10-15% of the total number of equivalent shares outstanding at any point in time. If the company has several classes of shares and/or warrants, the total number of equivalent shares is equal to the number of Common Shares that would exist if all classes of shares and all warrants were converted into Common Shares. The maximum number of Stock Options, whether issued or not, will increase over time due to successive financings, but the percentage will remain in the 10-15% range. Stock Options entitle the holder to purchase Common Shares at a fixed price. Stock Options vest, or become effective, incrementally over some period of time, and expire after some longer period of time or upon certain conditions. For example, a grant of Stock Options might vest at the rate of 25% per year beginning one year after, and expire seven years after, the date of issue. To exercise a Stock Option that has vested but not yet expired, the employee must pay the company an amount equal to the exercise price times the number of Stock Options being exercised, and in return will receive that same number of Common Shares. In private companies, the exercise price is usually the price investors paid in the company's most recently completed financing prior to the date the Stock Option was issued. The high potential value of Stock Options is due to the fact that the exercise price may be very low compared to the value of the Common Shares when the Stock Option is exercised.

The only hard and fast rule about Stock Options is this: the more important the employee, the more Stock Options. I believe it is best to make Stock Options available to all salaried employees, but not to hourly workers. In my experience, motivation through cash rewards for meeting goals under their control is the best incentive for hourly employees. Of the total option pool, 30% is reserved for a Stock Option grant that all eligible employees receive. The number of Stock Options an eligible employee receives is a percentage of starting salary. For most employees, those whose value to the company increases at an average rate, these are the only Stock Options they will receive. Additional Stock Options are not awarded when an employee receives a salary increase but may be awarded for exceptional performance. The remaining 70% of the option pool is allocated as follows: 30% as incentive grants for key employees, 30% as incentive grants for senior management, and 10% for contingencies.

The percentage of salary used to calculate the initial grant is determined by dividing the number of Stock Options available for this purpose by total annual payroll prior to the *next* anticipated financing. In the case of New Products Corporation, the Board has set the total pool at 10% of the number of equivalent shares. At the completion of its fourth year of operations and after it has arranged a bridge loan, there are 2,500,000 Common Shares, 1,333,333 Series A Preferred Shares, and a warrant that can be converted into 666,667 Common Shares, therefore the total number of Stock Options for eligible employees is 30% of 10% of 4,500,000: 135,000 Stock Options. If New Products Corporation expects its total annual payroll (excluding hourly workers) prior to the *next* anticipated financing, the mezzanine round, will be $3 million, then the percentage of salary to be used is 135,000 divided by 3,000,000, or 4.5%. Therefore, an employee with a gross salary of $30,000 per year would receive a grant of 1,350 Stock Options.

The next 30% or 135,000 Stock Options are reserved for incentive grants to key employees. These grants are in addition to the salary-based Stock Options received by all eligible employees. You need to be extremely careful with grants from this pool or you will run out of Stock Options before you have completed the task of building your organization. A rule of thumb is to limit grants from this pool in proportion to the expected number of years until the next financing round. If the next financing round is expected in two years, then 67,500 Stock Options can be awarded as incentives each year.

The remaining 30% or 135,000 Stock Options are reserved for senior management. I would parcel these out with grants of 27,000 each for the Chief Executive Officer, Chief Financial Officer and Chief Operating Officer, and 18,000 each for the Vice President Sales, Vice President Engineering and the Vice President Manufacturing. These grants are in addition to the salary-based Stock Options received by all eligible employees. In most companies, the Chief Executive Officer has a much larger block of Stock Options. My preference is for the senior management to share a little more equally in the upside, but my point of view is definitely in the minority. If you like to be part of the majority, do a little reallocation on your own behalf.

There is more to Stock Options than simply issuing them. In fact, if Stock Options are not presented in the appropriate manner, they can have an effect opposite to that intended. The first thing to consider is this: when you give an employee a grant of Stock Options you are usually giving it to two people, one of whom you may never have met. Your employee's spouse or significant other has an equal stake in the future value of the Stock Options. He or she has probably heard old stories about employees of startup companies who made small fortunes on their Stock Options, and newer stories about employees at other companies who received nothing but sheaves of worthless paper in return for their dedicated efforts. These tales are probably the sum total of what spouses, and sometimes your employees as well, know about the subject.

It is important to communicate the facts about Stock Options to everyone with a vested interest. Hold a meeting on the subject for employees and spouses. Your job is to explain the Employee Stock Option Plan in clear, understandable language. Then ask for questions. An evening such as this will be a real help in creating an atmosphere in the employee's home that is supportive of working late, out of town trips and the other inconveniences that working for a technology company sometimes bring to our personal lives and, based on the present direction of the company, will only increase in the future.

CHAPTER SEVENTEEN

Hiring an Investment Bank

*"When a fellow says it ain't the money but
the principal of the thing, it's the money."*
Abe Martin

Unless the fate of New Products Corporation is to become a
division of a much larger company, it is now on a trajectory of
growth and acquisitions leading to a future Initial Public Offering.
At some point before its IPO, the company will most likely need
to raise additional capital. Beginning with this mezzanine round
of financing, the company will take its search for capital to
professional investors across the country. These potential sources
of capital will include private equity funds, venture capital firms,
mutual funds, insurance companies, pension funds and high net
worth individuals. To effectively reach such a diverse group, future
company financings will be done through an intermediary financial
institution called an investment bank.

In contrast to the usual precision of the financial world, the
language used by the industry to describe itself is surprisingly
vague. An investment bank is not very much like a bank; it neither
accepts deposits nor makes loans. In a similar vein, most of the
employees of investment banks are not investment bankers. These
firms also employ brokers, traders, research analysts, an institutional
sales force, and a host of administrative people. Also, an investment
banker does not necessarily work for a company in the business of
buying and selling securities. Many investment bankers work for
boutique firms that provide specialized financial services for a fee.
To add to the confusion, some practitioners of the trade call

themselves merchant bankers, a terminology from Great Britain becoming increasingly popular on this side of the Atlantic.

For our purposes, an investment bank is an institution that represents companies issuing securities and an investment banker works in the corporate finance department of such a firm. Investment bankers are regarded, certainly by themselves, as the top guns of the financial world. Your venture capitalist will have existing relationships with a number of investment bankers, but what you require is more specific than that. If you begin placing calls to an arbitrary list of contacts, you will be drawn into an expanding, non-productive web of phone tag with the wrong people because, unless your business is located in San Francisco or New York, there will be a limited number of investment banks with experience in private equity financings for technology companies. Your task is to make a list of the investment banks that handle mezzanine round financings and obtain references to the Managing Director for private equity at each of these firms.

In this case, a "reference" is not much more than a name. With the right four or five names in hand, leave four or five messages something like this: "I'm the Chief Executive Officer of New Products Corporation. KBF Capital Partners have provided our venture capital financing. To support our rapidly growing business, we plan a $10 million mezzanine financing. Would it be possible for you to visit our company for an introductory meeting? I'd like to explain our story and find out more about your firm. If I'm not in, ask for my assistant who has my calendar and can set up a date and time."

You will get the meeting and they will come to you. Investment bankers are extremely aggressive and always on the hunt for a deal. Any legitimate-sounding company planning to raise $10 million is a company they want to see. At the introductory meetings, the Managing Director for private equity and one or two associates will be in a selling mode. They will be selling their services to you, explaining how highly their firm is ranked and the deals they have completed. Unless your company is a real dog, every word you speak will be met with praise and confirmation.

Don't let it go to your head. Whether the product is real estate or an investment banking assignment, the initial phase of a big-ticket sale follows an identical course. In the beginning the customer is always right. The sale can never be consummated until the seller has won over the buyer. Unlike real estate, however, in this case the desirability of making the sale is not a foregone conclusion. During a few weeks of polite meetings and friendly telephone calls, the Managing Director will be making the very serious decision to either commit resources to the financing project or to walk away. At the same time, you will be making a similar decision. The fate of your company will be in the hands of the investment bank that handles the financing. And so you and the Managing Director will enter an unaccustomed arena, not unlike the world of courting spiders, where both parties want to make the deal yet there are reasons to be wary.

More often than not, the investment bank you least prefer will make the first move and submit an Engagement Letter. Your job is to immediately contact the other investment banks and advise that the company has received an offer for consideration by the Board. With any luck, additional Engagement Letters will be forthcoming. The form of the Engagement Letter can vary widely, but at a minimum lists the principal terms upon which the investment bank proposes to act on behalf of the company.

By the time your Board of Directors formally convenes to consider the Engagement Letters, there will be a consensus. Of the offers, there is always one that stands out, but not for the reasons you might expect. The process may seem like a bidding war in which the best offer received is the one that will be accepted, but the reality of the situation is different. In almost every case, the investment bank that gets the deal is the most prestigious firm to make an offer. There may be a minor negotiation to deal with, for example an attempt to decrease the proposed fee by a percent or two, but the highest-ranking bank providing an Engagement Letter usually gets the deal.

The rationale for this state of affairs is this: the most important terms of the Engagement Letter, those dealing with deal structure,

World Wide Securities Inc. ("WWSI") confirms its interest to act as exclusive agent on a best efforts basis in connection with the proposed private placement offering of preferred shares by New Products Corporation ("NPC") on the terms outlined below. The

Issuer:	New Products Corporation.
Agent:	World Wide Securities Inc.
Amount of Issue:	Approximately $10 million
Pricing:	Pre-issue fully diluted valuation of approximately $20 million.
Closing Date:	(Approximately 12-14 weeks)
Securities:	Class "B" Preferred Shares
Conversion:	Convertible, at the option of the holder, into Common Shares on a one-for-one basis, or automatically upon the completion of a Qualified Initial Public Offering with gross proceeds of not less than $25 million.
Liquidation:	The holders of Class "B" Preferred Shares shall be entitled to receive in preference to all other classes of shares, in the event of liquidation of NPC at a value less than the price paid for the Class "B" Preferred Shares, an amount equal to the price pa
Agent's fee:	The agent will receive a commission equal to 7% of the gross proceeds of the offering.
Exclusivity:	During the term of the Agency Agreement, NPC agrees that WWSI will act as its exclusive financial advisor in connection with the offering.
Expenses:	NPC will be responsible for the costs and expenses of WWSI for the offering including legal fees, printing costs, out-of-pocket, travel and accommodation expenses.

Table 5. The Engagement Letter

have no real meaning. The deal structure proposed in the Engagement Letter is merely an indication of what the investment bank may consider possible. As is stated clearly in the Engagement Letter, the terms are subject to "completion of due diligence" which is an euphemism for "we'll see what a lead investor is prepared to offer." In a private equity financing the real terms are unknown at this point in time. The final terms will be negotiated, not between the company and the investment bank but between the company and the lead investor. These final terms will not necessarily be similar to those in the Engagement Letter.

In any event, chances are the deal structure outlined in the Engagement Letter will be acceptable. By the time the investment bank has decided they want the deal, they believe they can sell the deal and they have a good idea of your expectations in terms of pricing. In its own independent manner, the investment bank will analyze your company in terms of discounted future value and comparables and—surprise—they will come up with an answer acceptable to you. In short, if they want the deal, for the time being they will propose an acceptable valuation.

CHAPTER EIGHTEEN

The Mezzanine Round

"Money is always there, but the pockets change."
Gertrude Stein

The investment bankers will compose a detailed agenda of the milestones that must be accomplished in the twelve to fourteen weeks between the first meeting of the working group and the closing of the offering. The working group will include the executive management of the company and, from the investment bank there will be the Managing Director for private equity, two or three associates, and representatives from the firm's equity research department. The lawyers representing the company and the investment bank will contribute two or three people each, bringing the total working group to about fifteen members. As its first item of business, the working group will spend three weeks, and sometimes longer, condensing everything of importance about the company into the Private Placement Memorandum (PPM).

The Private Placement Memorandum, in its role as the authorized description of anything and everything a prospective investor needs to know, serves four purposes. The first two, a legal description of the company and an exhaustive compilation of every conceivable risk associated of the prospective investment, will be the responsibility of the lawyers but will be reviewed by all the members of the working group. The third purpose, to accurately present the company's financial information, is the responsibility of the Chief Financial Officer but will be reviewed by the company's accountants. The final purpose of the PPM is to describe the business of the company.

The Business of the Company section is the most difficult, and frustrating, to complete. While the story is your primary responsibility, every member of the group will have a hand in its content and composition. From the lawyers, you will learn there are very few statements of fact that do not require the qualification "in the opinion of management." From your investment bankers, you will learn there is very little you can say about your business that cannot benefit from gross oversimplification and a flow chart or illustration. There will be endless discussions about trivial points of grammar, content, format and sentence structure. Finally, after hours upon hours of committee work at a combined billing rate of thousands of dollars per hour, you will circulate a draft, receive comments from your Board of Directors, and start over again from the beginning.

The completed Private Placement Memorandum will look something like this:

- The Summary: written last but read first is usually a point-form rendition of the terms of the offering, company description, investment highlights and selected financial information. The Summary is intended to get the investor's attention therefore the more succinct the better. Aim for less than three pages.
- The Business of the Company: this is the meat of the document that, unfortunately, will not be read unless you have first captured the attention of the investors with a concise and engaging Summary.

   o   *The Industry* describes the market for your products, replete with pie charts and other graphics, in terms of size, growth and future trends.
   o   *Technology* reviews the company's intellectual property with the emphasis on how, through simplification or reduced cost, the company's patented technology provides a competitive advantage.

○ The *Products* section, illustrated with color photographs, portrays the company's products as solutions that incorporate the highly competitive technology described in the *Technology* section to address the market growth explained in the *Industry* section.

○ The *Future Products* section describes how the company plans to address new opportunities that will arise due to the future trends mentioned earlier.

○ *Customers* comprise an overview section describing well-known companies that have purchased or use the company's products.

○ *Customer Case Studies* detail examples of important customers that have designed-in the company's products and will, by inference, be high volume purchasers in the future.

○ *Business Model* explains how the company will take its innovative products into increasingly larger markets while, at the same time, will increase its margins.

○ *Growth Strategy* addresses the initiatives the company expects to employ to increase its revenue such as expansion of sales offices into new territories, an increase of sales to original equipment manufacturers, or an emphasis on emerging markets.

○ A section on *Sales and Marketing* describes marketing initiatives and sales channels, and includes graphics illustrating the responsibilities of the business units.

○ *Research and Development* presents the prior technology development successes of the company in the context of continuing future advancements.

○ *Intellectual Property* reviews issued and pending patents, and the company's trademark and copyright positions.

    ○   *Competition* points out the company's competitive advantages and discloses its principal competitors.

    ○   Finally, sections on *Human Resources* and *Facilities* disclose basic facts about personnel and floor space.

- It is becoming increasingly common for Private Placement Memorandums to include a forecast. The principal risk of including a forecast is it sets the stage for a lead investor to propose terms that are linked to achievement of the forecast. If at all possible, resist the inclusion of a forecast in the PPM.
- The document concludes with mandatory information including:

    ○   Directors and management,

    ○   Financial Statements,

    ○   Management's discussion and analysis of operating results,

    ○   Capitalization,

    ○   Share capital,

    ○   Employee Stock Option Plan,

    ○   Principal shareholders,

    ○   Use of proceeds,

    ○   Executive compensation,

    ○   Risk factors,

    ○   Material contracts,

    ○   And a few sections of legal boilerplate modified to the particulars of your company.

As the Private Placement Memorandum takes shape, a number of activities are going on behind the scenes. The accountants are double-checking every number. The lawyers are wrestling over the final form of pages of legalese. The associates at your investment bank are pounding the phones, lining up meetings with institutional investors. And, most importantly, you are rehearsing the road show presentation to selected members of the investment bank's equity sales team.

Finally, the Private Placement Memorandum is finished and, at a meeting of your Board of Directors, the document is formally approved. You and the Chief Financial Officer attended the meeting by conference telephone, from a boardroom at the investment bank that has been your office for the better part of a week. Since early that morning, you have been huddled with the Managing Director for private equity and senior associates. A two-week itinerary through the country's major financial centers, with each day divided into ninety-minute time slots, has been carefully constructed. The goal is to make between thirty and forty presentations in ten days including travel time.

It is during the road show that you learn a fundamental truth about corporate finance. Investment bankers are in the business of marketing, not sales. The old adage, that marketing is identical to sales except in marketing you don't have to ask for the order, is exactly right. The job of the investment banker is to get you in front of the client. Your job is to close the sale. But unlike a traditional selling job, you need to convince the customer without quoting a price. Because the terms will not exist until a lead investor issues a Term Sheet, you are selling something without a price.

The absence of a price is not necessarily a disadvantage. By quoting a price for something that is subject to negotiation, you effectively set the high water mark to investors who are very interested and a reason to walk away to investors with marginal interest. But without a set price, in a good market you can beat the price you want and in a bad market you can keep more potential investors engaged in the process. The strategy of not indicating a price can help your investment banker build a multiple bidding environment that is driven by the potential investors' perceptions of valuation.

Most retail investors believe that facts drive valuation. This view is especially palatable for those among us who see the world in terms of cause and effect. A stock is high because the company did this. The markets went up because the Fed cut rates. Everything has a reason because everything has to have a reason. And the reasons that matter most, therefore the ones that drive valuation, are in a one-to-one correspondence with the known facts. However intellectually satisfying this view may be, in the real world valuation is not the result of a mathematical calculation. It is not primarily based on facts, but on two entirely different entities: emotion and perception.

The values of publicly traded stocks are driven up and down by the emotions of fear and greed. Fearful investors sell and greedy investors buy. These same emotions have an impact on the value of a private company seeking to raise capital, but even more so. For example, if management does not perform, shareholders in publicly traded companies can sell their shares, take their losses, and move on. It is a completely different situation for shareholders in private companies. Unless management performs, shareholders in private companies will probably lose their entire investments. When the dominant emotion of the market is fear and investors seek liquidity above all else, private companies have little value and it is almost impossible for them to raise equity.

After emotion, the second factor driving valuation is perception. The price investors are willing to pay for shares in your company depends upon what investors perceive about your company. Investors can learn about the history of the company from the written material, but however wonderful the company's past performance may have been, investors are primarily concerned with the ability of management to deliver future performance. The word "liquidity" is constantly at the back of their minds and, since only the performance of management can deliver liquidity, investment decisions will be based more than anything else on the investors' perceptions of the chief executive. Your job is to repeatedly deliver a relatively short presentation that convinces investors you have the leadership skills, the stamina, the knowledge of the opportunities and challenges, the experience to make good decisions, and the abiding determination to succeed.

As you and your Chief Financial Officer are led through day after day of presentations, taxis, airports and conference calls, you can take comfort in the knowledge that your efforts are burying the investment bankers under a pile of work. For every ninety-minute presentation, you create a growing backlog for the investment bankers. It is their job to follow-up each presentation with phone calls, faxes and fat envelopes of additional materials sent by overnight courier.

Eventually, there will be a Term Sheet. If the process has gone exceptionally well, the Term Sheet will arrive before the road show has ended. This is nirvana for the investment banker because a Term Sheet received before the end of the road show means there is momentum. Deals close fast when there is momentum. But, more realistically, the Term Sheet comes after the road show. At this point, it's a matter of persistence. At the right price, you can usually find an investor with an interest. In a typical mezzanine round financing, the investment bankers go back to the potential lead investors several times before a Term Sheet is obtained. The Term Sheet will be sent by the lead investor to the investment bank, from them to you, and from you to your Board of Directors. The Term Sheet will outline a set of proposed terms for an investment in Series B Preferred Shares. Chances are there will be a number of terms unacceptable to your Board of Directors. Your venture capital partner, as the sole holder of Series A Preferred Shares, will be a forceful defender of the existing pecking order. The most contentious issues have to do with the conversion and liquidation rights of the new class of shares.

The Term Sheet illustrated in Table 6 is rife with provisions that may be found unacceptable to your Board of Directors. The Liquidation Value is very high. From the point of view of the company, the Liquidation Value should be closer to the price originally paid. A premium of two times the original price might be acceptable, but three times is excessive. Nevertheless, in spite of my opinion, in the present environment (2003) excessive Liquidation Values are often the case. As the Term Sheet is written, upon Liquidation the Purchasers are entitled to receive the Liquidation Value and then convert into Common Shares, therefore they will also receive part of any distribution to Common Shareholders. This demand, termed "double dipping," is becoming widespread.

Issuer	New Products Corporation
Purchasers	Sunrise Ventures Incorporated ("SVI"), KBF Capital Partners ("KBF"), and other investors (collectively "Purchasers")
Offering size	$10 million, of which SVI will invest $5 million and KBF $2 million
Securities to be acquired	2,247,191 Series B Convertible Redeemable Preferred Stock (the "Series B Preferred")
Price per share	$4.45
Use of proceeds	To provide working capital to fund growth and product development
Ranking	The Series B Preferred will rank senior to all other classes of equity with respect to the payment of Dividends, Redemption and upon Liquidation.
Liquidation	In the event of a Liquidation, change in control, merger or consolidation, the Purchasers will receive $13.35 (the "Liquidation Value") for each Series B Preferred plus accrued and unpaid Dividends prior to any payments being made to any other equity hold
Dividends	The Series B Preferred shareholders will be entitled to receive Dividends at a compounded annual rate of 8% and subject to proportional adjustment to reflect share splits.
Redemption	If the Company has not completed a Qualified Initial Public Offering ("QIPO") within three years, Purchasers have the right to receive the Liquidation Value of the Series B Preferred. A QIPO is an initial public offering resulting in proceeds to the Compa
Conversion	At the option of the Purchasers, the Series B Preferred is convertible at any time into Common Shares on a 1 to 1 basis, subject to adjustments for standard anti-dilution provisions.
Forced Conversion	The Series B Preferred will automatically be converted upon the completion of a QIPO.
Dividends on Conversion	Upon Conversion, accrued and unpaid Dividends shall be converted into Common Shares, based on the Series B Purchase Price adjusted for share splits.

Table 6. Mezzanine Round Term Sheet

The directors will insist that Liquidation and Conversion be decoupled, in other words under defined conditions the Purchasers may elect either the Liquidation or Conversion route but not both. Dividends are normally paid upon Liquidation, but not upon Conversion. The high Liquidation Value coupled with the fact that any change in control or merger can trigger its payment, places the Purchasers in a very powerful position. In addition, the definition of a QIPO at $50 million in proceeds is unrealistic for a company at this stage. $25 million is about right. The time limit puts the company in the position that in three years, unless it has completed a QIPO, the Purchasers will in effect own the company.

It is at this point that your investment bank can provide a service that helps justify its fee. Make a list of the issues and ask the investment bank to go back to the lead investor, but only in their capacity as agent, to negotiate some of the least desirable points out of the Term Sheet. The investment bank can take the position they want to clean up the offer before presenting it to the company's Board of Directors. This is a valuable service to the company because if there is going to be a dispute it will be between the investment bank and the lead investor not between the company and the lead investor. And, since the investment bank acted not for the company but in their capacity as agent, it remains appropriate for the Board of Directors to ask for changes after the lead investor issues version two of the Term Sheet.

After the Board of Directors approves the Term Sheet and the Chief Executive Officer signs it back to the lead investor, the investment bank circulates copies to the larger group of financial investors. Leading the due diligence process and setting the price and terms of the transaction are the responsibility of the lead investor. The financial investors will tag along and contribute not much more than their money to the process. Due diligence will include a rather extensive review of the company's affairs. The process will be conducted by one set of lawyers representing the lead investor and another representing the investment bank. A third set of lawyers, your own, will shuttle the documents back and forth. The company, in addition to paying for three sets of lawyers, is responsible for assembling a voluminous collection of information in a process called setting up a data room. The data room will contain every imaginable bit of written material that the three sets of lawyers might need to consult during the due diligence process.

The data room will contain the company's minute book including the articles of incorporation, by-laws, shareholder register, securities register, transfer register, directors register, officers list, all minutes and resolutions, the Employee Stock Option Plan, and shareholders' resolutions. The required financial information includes all quarterly and annual Financial Statements, a list of capital assets, copies of all banking documents, a current statement of accounts receivable and accounts payable, payroll and withholding information, and the company's Operational Plan. Sales and marketing information will include the sales pipeline, copies of significant customer orders, and any partnership or development agreements. Legal agreements will include investor agreements, agreements from previous financings, employee contracts, advisor agreements, warranty agreements, Confidential Disclosure Agreements, patents, patent applications and wrappers, materials relating to trademarks and copyrights, and all leases on premises, automobiles and equipment. The lawyers will also want to see copies of investor presentations, and the biographies of the officers and directors

By the time the due diligence process has been completed, in about two to three weeks, the investment bankers will have completed the book of participating investors. A short time later, there will be a closing similar to that following the venture capital round. This time, however, many more file folders will be strewn across the boardroom table.

CHAPTER NINETEEN

The Initial Public Offering

"Don't buy your own poster."
Advice from my wife Diane

For the last twenty years, the public company has been king.
Success has been measured in terms of growth and name
recognition, rather than stability and profitability, and a good story
has frequently been worth more than a good product. It was all
about buying, not building; about the top line, not the bottom
line; and about the next quarter, the next acquisition, and the next
spin-off. To many chief executives and their boards, stock price
was king, earnings were secondary, and dividends were for suckers.
"Greed is good", Gordon Gekko's memorable line from Oliver
Stone's 1987 film *Wall Street*, became the mantra of the best and
the brightest. It was an environment in which new companies
remained private for the shortest possible period of time. Going
public with a listing on a major stock exchange was the consummate
symbol of achievement, and the goal of every greenhorn
entrepreneur.

How times have changed in a few short years. Yesterday, the
majority of new public companies had not yet made a profit. Today,
it is practically impossible to take an unprofitable company public.
Yesterday, the emphasis was to make money by taking the company
public. Today the emphasis is to make money by building a
profitable company. Today, as was the case yesterday, the minimum
threshold of achievement before a company is ready for its Initial
Public Offering moves up and down according to the dominant
sentiment of the financial markets. When the "window is wide

open," meaning the new issues market is hot, it is possible for relatively junior technology companies to complete Initial Public Offerings. But when the window closes, even the largest and best performing companies may be unsuccessful. In October 2001, when no technology company completed an Initial Public Offering in North America, for the first time in many years the window was nailed shut. Most of the time, however, the window is partially opened. In these average times, a typical IPO candidate has achieved a high rate of growth and will exceed $20 million in revenue for the current year. Profitability is not as important as revenue and growth, but the company should be on an earnings trajectory with the top line growing faster than expenses. If the company also exhibits a record of gradually increasing operating margins, that will be interpreted as a sign of good management, always a bonus.

Public companies are slotted into a hierarchy. At the top of the pecking order are the components of the Dow Jones Industrial Average and the NASDAQ 100, the leading companies of the premier stock exchanges. These few companies are at the top of the heap, unlisted public companies are at the bottom, and the rest of the public company universe are somewhere in between. New public companies don't enter this hierarchy at the top, but many enter at or near the bottom. Your job is to position your company as far up the list as possible.

For most of its long history beginning in 1817, the New York Stock Exchange stood alone as foremost in the country. The early technology companies such as Texas Instruments and IBM listed on the venerable exchange. The rise of NASDAQ began midway though the semiconductor revolution. Starting with Intel in 1971, an increasing number of public technology companies have opted for NASDAQ. Today we have two prestigious stock exchanges, but the destination of choice for technology companies is usually NASDAQ. NASDAQ stands for "National Association of Securities Dealers Automated Quotation System" and, as the longer name implies, NASDAQ is an electronic stock market. Without a centralized trading floor, securities are bought and sold over a high-speed computer network linking more than a million users in more than eighty countries. Over four thousand public companies are listed on NASDAQ. Within the NASDAQ system, there are two levels of listed companies: the NASDAQ National Market and the NASDAQ Small Cap Market.

To be eligible for inclusion in the NASDAQ National Market, a company must meet a specific set of eligibility requirements. The requirements include a $5 minimum stock price, at least 400 shareholders, and a minimum—depending on the eligibility rule used to qualify for listing—of either three or four market makers. A market maker is an employee of an investment dealer who posts and supports a bid and ask price for the stock. In addition to these standard qualifications, the company must fulfill any one of three sets of eligibility rules that can be summarized by the business development stage of the applicant: for profitable companies, pre-tax income (not net income) must exceed $1 million; for established companies, annual revenue, total assets or market capitalization, must exceed $75 million; and for growth companies, net tangible assets must exceed $18 million. This last is the usual eligibility criteria for a new public technology company because, flush with cash from the Initial Public Offering, net tangible assets should exceed $18 million.

To list on the NASDAQ Small Cap Market a company must have a minimum stock price of $4, at least 300 shareholders, and a minimum of three market makers. There are additional requirements that can also be summarized by the business development stage of the applicant: for profitable companies, net income (not pre-tax income) must exceed $750,000; for established companies, market capitalization must exceed $50 million; and for growth companies, net tangible assets must exceed $4 million.

All companies that are listed on a stock exchange are public companies, but not all public companies are listed on a stock exchange. Many of the companies that fall into this category are formerly listed companies that failed to maintain listing requirements, but there are also a large number of public companies that have never been listed on a stock exchange. Simply becoming a public company is not a difficult procedure; the trick is to become a listed public company. If the extent of your ambition is merely to be public, the usual procedure is to file a form SB2 acceptable to the Securities and Exchange Commission. Once public, subject to regulatory policies including rules governing eligible investors, there are markets for shares in companies not listed on an exchange.

NASDAQ operates a quotation service for such companies. The OTC Bulletin Board consists of unlisted public companies in which market makers maintain a level of liquidity by supporting a posted bid and ask price. Application for inclusion on the OTC Bulletin Board is made through a market maker and there are no listing requirements other than the company must file certain reports with the Securities and Exchange Commission. Shares in other unlisted public companies are regularly traded through the "Pink Sheets" which are weekly quotations printed on pink paper by Pink Sheets LLC. There is also an electronic version of the Pink Sheets that is updated daily.

An underwriter is defined as an intermediary that purchases shares from the company prior to distribution to the public. The shares are purchased at a discount to the offering price, known as the spread, of between four to seven percent. Until public buyers purchase the stock, the underwriter owns the shares. Supposedly, the underwriter deserves its sizable spread because of the cost and risk of taking ownership of the shares. In the IPO market, however, the reality is the underwriter usually makes no firm commitment until the offering has been pre-sold. The period of time between the transfer of title to the underwriter and the transfer of title from the underwriter is so short only corporate lawyers can comprehend its brevity. At the same time, a growing number of Initial Public Offerings aren't underwritten at all but are on a "best efforts" basis where, unlike ordinary mortals who own something before they sell it, the underwriter in fact never owns the shares. Regardless of these fine points, the investment banker in the process of managing an Initial Public Offering is called an underwriter whether or not the financing is underwritten.

Your investment banker from the mezzanine round will argue that the relationship between the issuer and the underwriter of the Initial Public Offering is of such importance that the company would be ill-advised to change its investment bank at this late stage of the game. But the argument is fallacious. In the financial world it is self-interest, not time, that is the best determinant of an important relationship. On Wall Street, important relationships can form in a New York minute. Having made it onto the radar screens of numerous investment bankers during the mezzanine round, there will be no shortage of investment banks willing to act as underwriter and take you public.

Selecting an underwriter is similar to the process leading up to the mezzanine round. There will be a stream of meetings, "beauty contests," at which the investment banks make their case for being the best-qualified firm to underwrite your Initial Public Offering. Eventually, you will receive the first Offer to Finance and then the other competitors will follow suit. Again, it will be up to your Board of Directors to make the final decision, but the highest-ranking firm providing an Offer to Finance usually gets the deal. An exception to the rule of the highest-ranking firm occurs when one of the investment banks agrees to act as an underwriter in the traditional sense of the word. An investment bank offering to assume the risk of successful completion, as opposed to working on a best efforts basis, automatically jumps to the top of the queue.

The negotiation process is usually confined to the issue of compensation and, once upon a time, the process ended when the percentage fee was agreed. Now there is also the additional issue of the over-allotment option. The first company that was sold this particular bill of goods was the Green Shoe Manufacturing Company of Boston, Massachusetts, during its 1960 Initial Public Offering. The Green Shoe Manufacturing Company, founded in 1918, has since changed its name to Stride Rite Corporation and continues to manufacture shoes. But the name "Green Shoe" lives on as standard investment industry jargon for the over-allotment option.

A typical Green Shoe is 15%, meaning the underwriter receives the option to sell up to 115% of the number of shares purportedly available for sale. For a period of sixty days from closing, the underwriter may purchase up to 15% more than the base number of shares on the same terms as the Initial Public Offering. Ideally, the Green Shoe helps stabilize the market in the period immediately following the IPO. In this scenario, the underwriter sells 115% of the issue prior to closing. At closing, the company delivers the base number of shares to the underwriter and receives payment for the base number of shares. The missing 15% does not yet exist in the form of issued shares, but merely as cash in the underwriter's bank account. In the event the company's shares decline below issue price during the sixty days following the IPO, the underwriter uses all or part of the cash to buy back shares, thereby stabilizing the market. At the end of the sixty-day period, the remaining cash is converted into shares at a "second closing" and the newly issued shares are distributed to their respective owners.

The Green Shoe can have a positive impact by providing a measure of stability to the market immediately following the IPO. If the stock does poorly, the underwriter will buy back shares (stabilizing the market) at prices no higher than the IPO price. If the buy back price is lower then the IPO price, the underwriter makes a profit. For every share bought back, one fewer share needs to be purchased when and if the Green Shoe is exercised. If the stock rises, the underwriter exercises the Green Shoe but keeps the accrued interest. Either way, the underwriter makes money and takes on zero risk. To the underwriter, it's like a short sale without any obligation to cover your losses. Whether or not your Board of Directors has a strong opinion on the subject, chances are the Offer to Finance will include an over-allotment option.

The first gathering of the parties will be the "all hands meeting" which will be attended by a large contingent from the underwriter, underwriter's counsel, company management, and the company's lawyers and auditors. The purpose of the meeting is supposedly planning, but the gathering is chiefly symbolic. The world of investment banking, however ruthless and uncaring it may be, is steeped in tradition. Meetings like the all hands meeting strike a balance, somewhere between duty to the client and reverence to the firm, to which senior investment bankers aspire. The meeting provides an opportunity for the corporate finance team to distribute a timetable including action items and responsibilities, and for company management to meet senior management of the investment bank.

After the all hands meeting, the first item of business is writing the Preliminary Prospectus. If you enjoyed writing the Private Placement Memorandum, you will find this procedure even more enchanting. It's the same iterative process of drafting, reviewing, nitpicking, re-drafting, then circulating the results only to start all over again, that you have come to know and love. From the legal point of view, the Preliminary Prospectus is a more formal description of the company than the Private Placement Memorandum. It follows the same outline but with additional legal boilerplate and a higher level of financial disclosure. Three years of audited Financial Statements (less if the company has been in business fewer than three years) are required plus interim Financial Statements for each quarter since the end of the last fiscal year. The Preliminary Prospectus, known in SEC lingo as form S1, is the first in a series of documents a public company must file on a regular basis. Examples of this and other filings can be downloaded from the SEC website.

While the working group is busy with the Preliminary Prospectus, the underwriter, acting as "lead manager" forms a "syndicate," with the guidance of the company, of investment banks that will jointly distribute the offering. Investment banks are very competitive but out of necessity they work together. Your underwriter may rightly claim the syndicate is formed for the benefit of the issuer because distributing the offering as widely as possible is to the benefit of the company. But if your underwriter claims syndication (with its consequent fee-splitting) proves the interests of the client come first, they have gone too far. The real reason for syndication is twofold: it is easier to complete financings that are syndicated, and forming syndicates have no real impact on fees. Underwriters keep records of whom they bring in and who brings them in, and, over time, get back as much as they give away. Each member of the syndicate, the underwriting group, makes a commitment to distribute a percentage or "takedown" of the offering. The members of the syndicate may elect to sell their takedown through internal operations or they may arrange for outside brokerages to sell part of their allotment. The organizations that actually sell the shares to the public are called the "selling group."

As soon as the Preliminary Prospectus, also known as a Registration Statement, has been completed it is filed with the Securities and Exchange Commission. The Preliminary Prospectus is called a "red herring" because of the legends printed in red ink on the cover. Subject to changes required by the SEC, it is identical to the final prospectus except the number of shares to be sold, the pricing of the shares, the underwriting amount, and any reference derived from these three quantities is "bulleted." A line from the description of share capital might read, "After giving effect to this issue, • Common Shares will be issued and outstanding."

After filing, a twenty-day "cooling off period" begins. During the cooling off period members of the selling group are prohibited from sending any materials to prospective investors other than the Preliminary Prospectus. This activity is not considered selling. It is not legal to accept orders until a security has cleared registration by the SEC. Instead, the underwriter compiles a book consisting of "indications of interest" expressed by prospective purchasers.

About thirty days after filing the Preliminary Prospectus, the SEC will respond with written comments. These comments or "deficiencies" need to be addressed by filing an amendment to the SEC. Once the amendment is filed, the road show and other selling efforts may begin. The SEC may issue additional written comments to the amendment and subsequent rounds of amendments until the SEC clears the Preliminary Prospectus. Clearing registration means the SEC has examined the documentation and has found it complete but does not imply that the SEC approves of the issue. A statement that the SEC has approved of an issue is a violation of federal law.

It is sensible to expect the senior investment bankers of the underwriter, people who make their living distributing securities, will be able to provide useful assistance in putting together your road show presentation. Nothing could be further from the truth. An underwriter believes there is but one way to "tell the story" and that is with a script and a canned presentation, either projected onto a screen for larger audiences or reduced to flip charts for the one-on-one meetings. They will insist you put together such a presentation and you will have to do it. In the rehearsals the underwriter will arrange, first to selected members of the working group and then to the underwriter's institutional sales group, you are well advised to follow the script that has been drawn up for you.

It's been said that all effective presentations conform to the same format: first tell them what you are going to tell them, next tell them, and finally tell them what you have told them. It's a great line, but not very helpful. Investors are the furthest thing away from a captive audience which is the only venue at which lecturing is appropriate. Investors are free creatures that first of all must be drawn into the excitement of the opportunity.

Get the attention of the investors at the beginning of the presentation and then hold it by explaining the story of your company with as much passion as you can muster. Use the facts and figures of the prepared presentation as a backdrop. Don't read the content of your slides to your audience, they can read the material faster than you can speak and, in any case, each investor receives a copy of the presentation. If you briefly summarize the contents of each slide in a measured and confident voice, you will be doing better than the majority of reader-presenters, but your finest moments will come when your comments add to the content of the prepared slides. For example, with a graphic representing sales in the Asia-Pacific region projected on the screen behind you, the story of how the company secured distribution in Japan and an explanation of why the company believes it is positioned to penetrate this important market, is an enrichment to the prepared material and hopefully interesting to the audience. If your anecdote elicits a reaction from the audience, a murmur of approval or laughter, you will glow for the rest of the day.

Any material statements about the company must be based

on facts disclosed in the Preliminary Prospectus. If you disclose material information not contained in the Preliminary Prospectus, you will be a two-time loser: for uttering the statement and also for not including the information in the Preliminary Prospectus. By law, the Preliminary Prospectus must disclose all material facts about the company. The same proviso applies to forward looking statements. It is permissible to talk about the future plans of the company, but only to the extent the plans have been disclosed, but forecasts are usually forbidden. The exception is when the Preliminary Prospectus contains a forecast that has been prepared under strict accounting guidelines, called "FOFI" for Future Oriented Financial Information, in which case you may discuss it to the extent it has been disclosed.

Unlike the road show of the mezzanine round with its constant stream of one-on-one meetings, a day on an IPO road show usually contains a number of group presentations. A typical day starts with a breakfast meeting with a small group of institutional investors, then a larger and more diverse group of investors attend a lunch sponsored by a member of the selling group, and after the stock market closes for the day there is an informal meeting with a room full of retail stock brokers. In between, there are one-on-one meetings with institutional investors and analysts.

Analysts are particularly important to the success of an Initial Public Offering because stock exchange listing requirements stipulate a minimum number of shareholders, 400 in the case of the NASDAQ National Market. Since the number of institutional investors will be relatively small, the IPO must also be sold to retail investors. It's also important to have retail investors because they provide liquidity through buying and selling the stock while institutional investors, because they tend to buy and hold, do not provide much liquidity. The direct channel to retail investors is through retail brokers. Large investment firms may employ thousands of retail brokers and these people will rely on a description of the company that has been written up by an analyst.

The major difference between presentations to analysts and presentations to investors is the quantity and quality of the questions that are asked. Analysts are experts. They know the questions to ask and they can understand the responses. When talking to an analyst, the best guideline is to leave some of your natural enthusiasm outside in the hallway. After a few years of listening to more good stories than a Hollywood producer, analysts learn to be deeply sceptical. But you can usually win over an analyst with technical detail and honesty. Try to preface your encouraging remarks with a personal assessment of the risks. For example you might say, "While there is a level of risk involved in scaling our process to higher quantities, we believe the technology is right and the risk is one of timing rather than something more fundamental."

Investment banker terminology for the IPO road show is the "marketing phase." It's a gruelling journey through airports, boardrooms, hotels and taxis. It takes you to a land of continuous presentations and one-on-one meetings that are indistinguishable from one another. To the road show participant, as the process interminably drags it seems like it will never end. Then everything happens at once.

At some magical point, the underwriter will decide that the book has grown to a sufficient size to allow the offering to close. With such a prospect in mind, the thoughts of the underwriter immediately turn from marketing the issue to the more practical issue of reducing the risk of future liability. A series of formal due diligence sessions are held in which the officers of the company answer questions about the accuracy of the information contained within the Preliminary Prospectus. The grand inquisitors are the lawyers representing the interests of the underwriter. What is of principal concern is to establish that the Preliminary Prospectus completely and accurately discloses all the material facts about the company and that no new material facts have arisen since the document was completed. Written minutes are taken and the officers of the company are warned they can be held personally liable for their answers. In the event the IPO investors lose money and sue everybody involved in the process, the written minutes will be used to protect the underwriter and place the blame squarely upon management.

The due diligence sessions are also attended by the company's auditors who are asked questions relating to the accuracy of the Financial Statements. The auditors, having long ago achieved mastery of this game, carefully explain how they have relied on information supplied by management. The auditors are happy to accept responsibility for the mathematical accuracy of the Financial Statements, but little else. Besides testifying at due diligence, the auditors are also required to provide a "comfort letter." In this document, the underwriter wants the auditors to say they have independently confirmed the financial information of the Preliminary Prospectus, they agree with the financial records of the company, and confirm that no material changes have occurred since the date of the Preliminary Prospectus. However, the comfort letter will be carefully drafted to limit liability, stating only that the auditors do not disagree with any of the statements made in the Preliminary Prospectus. Underwriters refer to this sort of tentative, convoluted opinion as a "cold comfort letter." The underwriter will insist on changes to the comfort letter and the auditors will respond with a second draft that will also fail to meet the requirements of the underwriters. At some point, after the process reaches true hopelessness, one of the parties in this game of brinkmanship will give in to the other.

As soon as the due diligence sessions have been completed and an acceptable comfort letter has been received from the auditor, the company is invited to sign the underwriting agreement. Pity the poor entrepreneur who has been laboring under the impression that the investment bank has been acting as its underwriter all along. In this bizarre world of finance it is only now, confident that the Initial Public Offering will close and comfortable with its liability, that the underwriter will commit in writing to act as the underwriter. The underwriting agreement spells out the terms and conditions of the underwriting exactly as they are disclosed in the Preliminary Prospectus.

Having signed the underwriting agreement, it's time for a second surprise. It's time to price the issue. One critical fact not contained in the Preliminary Prospectus, the price, has yet to be set. At times, this is the occasion taken by the underwriter to inform the company the price that had been informally understood for many months is too high. If this is one of those times, the blame for this sudden change of heart will be placed on an obscure high-level group at the investment bank known as "the committee" that ultimately is responsible for setting the price. But, happily, most of the time the price is the price.

At some point before pricing, the final amendments to the Preliminary Prospectus have been filed with the Securities and Exchange Commission and the document has been cleared and becomes effective. Immediately following pricing the Final Prospectus, in which the bullets of the Preliminary Prospectus are replaced with the actual quantities, is issued, and, three days after pricing the offering closes and the company receives the net proceeds. That's the theory, at least. There can be unexpected complications.

Depending on the type of listing sought, it may also be necessary for individual states to review your Preliminary Prospectus. If you qualify for the NASDAQ National Market or the New York Stock Exchange, then your IPO is not subject to review by the individual states. But if you plan to be listed on the NASDAQ Small Cap Market, your IPO materials are also subject to review and approval by regulators in other jurisdictions including every state where the offering will be sold.

Approval of a Preliminary Prospectus in multiple jurisdictions can involve serious complications. In 1995, the CRS Robotics Corporation Initial Public Offering was ready to close. All the board, shareholder and underwriter issues had been resolved. The Prospectus had been filed and reviewed by the principal regulator, and the comments and deficiencies had been satisfactorily addressed. The road show was over. There were sufficient indications of interest to expect the offering would be oversubscribed. We expected the deal to close at any moment. But this IPO required the approval of one more regulator.

As President of the company, my job was to keep everyone on side until the last few bits of paperwork were completed. Then, at the end of the final day, I got a call from the company's lawyer. A west coast jurisdiction had an issue and they were pressing for the issue to be resolved in a manner exactly opposite of what had already been agreed with the principal regulator. I went immediately to my lawyer's office and we began making telephone calls. At issue was a seemingly unimportant point that was contentious nonetheless. My lawyer, a brilliant negotiator by the name of Geoff Beattie, did most of the talking. First to one regulator, then to the other, he carefully explained how the company was caught in the middle. Having set the stage, he teleconferenced the parties together and, through irrefutable argument, forced them to resolve the impasse then and there. Shortly after, the CRS Robotics Corporation Initial Public Offering closed.

Once the IPO closes, the company's shares begin to trade on the stock exchange. The first 25 days of trading are called a "quiet period" during which the company and insiders must not make comments about the stock. Analysts typically begin coverage of companies after the quiet period ends. Finally, the underwriter will publish a "tombstone," a newspaper ad publicizing the fact that the offering has taken place and listing the members of the syndicate, with the lead underwriter receiving top billing.

APPENDIX

Practical Accounting and Forecasting

"The measure of success is not whether you have a tough problem to deal with, but whether it's the same problem you had last year"
John Foster Dulles

I got into serious financial trouble in the last quarter of 1984, but was blissfully unaware of the fact until February of the following year. That was when my Chief Financial Officer brought it to my attention with the words, "Our cash is being sucked into a black hole." Less than a year before, Varah Electronics had raised millions of dollars in its Initial Public Offering and had embarked on a period of growth that included an acquisition and several new sales offices. Until that Tuesday afternoon in February, with a draft of the annual Financial Statements spread out on my desk, I had thought the company, under my gifted and instinctive leadership, had been performing spectacularly. Instead, the indisputable numbers told the story of a company that had completely lost control of its cash. The numbers also revealed an uncomfortable truth. I didn't know how to manage my own company.

It took several quarters of intensive work to identify and correct the operational issues that were draining the company of its cash. During this period of time, I learned it is absolutely essential to understand the business of a company in financial terms in order to properly manage its affairs—but an understanding of Financial Statements is not enough. Far more important than knowledge of the past, is an understanding of the company's potential future. The purpose of the Operational Plan is to provide a useable financial model that predicts the future performance of a company.

The Operational Plan covers a 12-month period. In Table 7, Month 1 is the same as Month 7 in the Seed Round Financial Forecast of Table 1. Reading across the columns, the first four months present historical results and the last eight months comprise a forecast. The historical results are a restatement of the company's monthly Financial Statements, and the forecast is generated by assumptions that have been entered into a spreadsheet program. This format allows past performance to be used as a template for the future and, even more powerfully, allows the entrepreneur to understand the impact of decisions and strategies on future performance. By plugging assumptions into a working copy of the Operational Plan, the entrepreneur can immediately see the future financial impact of an increase in Raw Materials cost, or a change in interest rates, or a decrease in Sales, or a change in the collections rate.

The first page of the Operational Plan consists of the Income Statement. For each heading reading down the left side of the page, there are four monthly columns of "Actual" results and eight columns of "Forecast" estimates. The Sales number is the total amount sold and invoiced to customers during the month. Cost of Sales consists of Raw Materials and Direct Labor. Raw Materials, the component parts consumed in the manufacturing process, are the amount consumed in the month. During the forecast period, Raw Materials have been estimated as a percentage of Sales. The assumption is that the percentage will decline over time from 21% of Sales in May to 19% of Sales by December. Direct Labor is the total amount paid in salaries, hourly wages and benefits to manufacturing personnel. Unlike the Seed Round Financial Forecast that recorded all employee remuneration under Expenses, the Operational Plan only includes non-manufacturing employees under Expenses. In the forecast period, Direct Labor is expected to decrease from 23% to 18% as a percentage of Sales. The reduction in the cost of Direct Labor is due to, and begins in the months following, major investments in Capital Assets.

The "Actual" Expenses are copied from the company's monthly Financial Statements. The Expenses of the forecast period are the assumptions of management. For example, New Products Corporation plans to hire sales personnel in July, August and December, and therefore estimated Salaries and Benefits are entered in the corresponding periods. In addition, it is assumed that the sales personnel will be partially compensated by Commissions that will total about 1% of Sales. All of the Expenses are handled in a similar manner except Professional Fees. This category has been expensed on a straight-line basis. Professional Fees have been estimated to total $24,000 for the year. The monthly amount in the forecast period is the unspent portion of the $24,000, divided by the remaining number of months.

EBITDA stands for Earnings Before Interest Tax Depreciation and Amortization. EBITDA is frequently used to compare technology companies because, unlike the absolute bottom line of Earnings, EBITDA is independent of capitalization, and is therefore a useful measure of operational performance. In the case of New Products Corporation, Interest is a negative quantity because the company receives interest income. Depreciation and Amortization are the same thing except the former has to do with tangible assets, such as equipment, and the latter with intangible assets, such as a patent. The concept of Depreciation is best understood in terms of the impact of an investment in Capital Assets on the financial performance of a going concern over a period of several years. For example, take the case of a semiconductor company that builds a multi-million dollar fabrication facility. The company may very well spend an amount that exceeds its annual Earnings. Question: should the company show a huge loss for that year? Answer: of course not. The benefits of the new facility will be realized over a number of years, therefore the costs associated with the Capital Asset are charged as an expense over a number of years. The entire amount, say $500 million, was spent during the year to acquire the Capital Asset. But, for the purposes of the Income Statement, this total is divided by the expected number of years of useful life and that is the amount charged each year as an expense. In other words, Depreciation is an expense charged to the company for money long since spent. The rate at which Depreciation can be expensed depends

INCOME STATEMENT	ACTUAL Jan	ACTUAL Feb	ACTUAL Mar	ACTUAL Apr	FORECAST May
SALES	31,006	34,555	35,780	43,568	45,000
Cost of Sales:					
Materials	7,751	8,638	8,229	10,020	9,450
Direct Labor	7,098	7,025	7,120	9,210	10,350
GROSS PROFIT	16,157	18,892	20,431	24,338	25,200
Gross Margin	52.10%	54.70%	57.10%	55.90%	56.00%
EXPENSES:					
Salaries and Benefits:					
Operations	8,000	8,000	8,000	8,000	8,000
Sales	0	0	0	0	0
Engineering	4,000	4,000	4,000	4,000	4,000
Commissions	0	0	0	0	0
Product Development Expen.	0	0	0	0	0
Advertising and Promotion	0	0	0	0	0
Communications	865	884	568	799	1,000
Miscellaneous	1,210	569	584	981	1,000
Office Supplies	652	1,355	911	820	1,000
Professional Fees	358	8,914	0	0	1,841
Rent	3,000	3,000	3,000	3,000	3,000
Travel	0	560	866	2,144	1,000
Utilities	986	899	903	954	1,000
TOTAL EXPENSES	19,071	28,181	18,832	20,698	21,841
EBITDA	-2,914	-9,289	1,599	3,640	3,359
Interest costs	-188	-167	-115	-105	-107
Depreciation	1,064	1,087	1,065	1,044	1,024
Corporate Income Taxes	0	0	0	0	0
EARNINGS (LOSS)	-3,790	-10,209	649	2,701	2,442

Table 7. The Operational Plan—

FORECAST Jun	FORECAST Jul	FORECAST Aug	FORECAST Sep	FORECAST Oct	FORECAST Nov	FORECAST Dec
45,000	50,000	55,000	65,000	75,000	85,000	100,000
9,450	10,500	11,000	13,000	14,250	16,150	19,000
10,350	11,500	12,650	14,950	16,500	17,000	18,000
25,200	28,000	31,350	37,050	44,250	51,850	63,000
56.00%	56.00%	57.00%	57.00%	59.00%	61.00%	63.00%
8,000	8,000	8,000	8,000	10,000	10,000	12,000
0	3,500	7,000	7,000	7,000	7,000	10,500
4,000	4,000	4,000	7,000	7,000	7,000	7,000
0	500	550	650	750	850	1,000
0	0	1,000	1,000	1,000	1,000	1,000
0	500	500	1,000	1,000	2,000	2,000
1,000	1,200	1,400	1,600	1,800	2,000	2,000
1,000	1,000	1,000	1,000	1,000	1,000	1,000
1,000	1,000	1,000	1,000	1,000	1,000	1,000
1,841	1,841	1,841	1,841	1,841	1,841	1,841
3,000	3,000	3,000	3,000	3,000	3,000	3,000
1,000	1,000	2,000	2,000	2,000	3,000	3,000
1,000	1,000	1,000	1,000	1,000	1,000	1,000
21,841	26,541	32,291	36,091	38,391	40,691	46,341
3,359	1,459	-941	959	5,859	11,159	16,659
-93	-96	-1,989	-1,723	-799	-777	-763
1,004	984	3,416	12,172	11,934	11,700	12,451
0	0	0	0	0	0	0
2,448	571	-2,368	-9,490	-5,276	236	4,971

Income Statement

	ACTUAL Jan	ACTUAL Feb	ACTUAL Mar	ACTUAL Apr	FORECAST May
CASH FLOW					
OPENING BANK	93,674	83,455	57,381	52,241	53,121
Sources:					
Net Earnings	-3,790	-10,209	649	2,701	2,442
Depreciation	1,064	1,087	1,065	1,044	1,024
Accounts Payable	586	1,629	2,046	-1,003	4,773
Sale of Equity	0	0	0	0	0
Uses:					
Accounts Receivable	8,214	12,678	9,254	1,000	16,114
Raw Materials	-135	1,324	971	862	-829
Finished Goods	0	1,325	-1,325	0	0
Purchase of Capital Assets	0	3,254	0	0	0
CASH FLOW	-10,219	-26,074	-5,140	880	-7,046
CLOSING BANK	83,455	57,381	52,241	53,121	46,075
BALANCE SHEET					
ASSETS					
Bank	83,455	57,381	52,241	53,121	46,075
Accounts Receivable	49,522	62,200	71,454	72,454	88,568
Raw Materials	7,122	8,446	9,417	10,279	9,450
Finished Goods	0	1,325	0	0	0
Capital Assets	52,165	54,332	53,267	52,223	51,199
TOTAL ASSETS	192,264	183,684	186,379	188,077	195,292
LIABILITIES					
Accounts Payable	12,025	13,654	15,700	14,697	19,470
Shareholders' Equity:					
Capital Stock	320,000	320,000	320,000	320,000	320,000
Retained Earnings	-139,761	-149,970	-149,321	-146,620	-144,178
TOTAL LIABILITIES	192,264	183,684	186,379	188,077	195,292

Table 7. The Operational Plan—

FORECAST Jun	FORECAST Jul	FORECAST Aug	FORECAST Sep	FORECAST Oct	FORECAST Nov	FORECAST Dec
46,075	47,525	994,080	861,178	399,360	388,018	381,204
2,448	571	-2,368	-9,490	-5,276	236	4,971
1,004	984	3,416	12,172	11,934	11,700	12,451
-570	1,050	1,550	2,500	3,250	3,150	4,750
0	950,000	0	0	0	0	0
1,432	5,000	10,000	15,000	20,000	20,000	25,000
0	1,050	500	2,000	1,250	1,900	2,850
0	0	0	0	0	0	0
0	0	125,000	450,000	0	0	50,000
1,450	946,555	-132,902	-461,818	-11,342	-6,814	-55,678
47,525	994,080	861,178	399,360	388,018	381,204	325,526
47,525	994,080	861,178	399,360	388,018	381,204	325,526
90,000	95,000	105,000	120,000	140,000	160,000	185,000
9,450	10,500	11,000	13,000	14,250	16,150	19,000
0	0	0	0	0	0	0
50,195	49,210	170,795	608,622	596,688	584,989	622,538
197,170	1,148,790	1,147,973	1,140,982	1,138,956	1,142,343	1,152,064
18,900	19,950	21,500	24,000	27,250	30,400	35,150
320,000	1,270,000	1,270,000	1,270,000	1,270,000	1,270,000	1,270,000
-141,730	-141,160	-143,527	-153,018	-158,294	-158,057	-153,086
197,170	1,148,790	1,147,973	1,140,982	1,138,956	1,142,343	1,152,064

Cash Flow and Balance Sheet

on the Capital Asset being depreciated. New Products Corporation depreciates the value of its Capital Assets by 2% per month.

There is another side to the story of Depreciation. However rational the above explanation may sound, the real reason capital costs are expensed over an extended period is that governments have mandated the use of Depreciation. If governments allowed companies to deduct capital investments as ordinary expenses, tax receipts would plunge. Not only would governments have to wait for their money but also endure the risk that the company may not have the cash to pay its taxes in the future. The fact that the concept of non-cash expenses violates the essential symmetry of the Income Statement is, like death and taxes, something we must learn to accept.

The second page of the Operational Plan consists of the Cash Flow and the Balance Sheet. The Cash Flow is the most difficult section of ordinary Financial Statements because its usual format is alien to what a normal human might expect. If the Income Statement contains an error, a reasonably intelligent individual can usually locate the problem through application of diligence and common sense. Not so with the Cash Flow. If the Income Statement is clarity, the Cash Flow is befuddlement. In its usual format, this statement is divided into three equally bewildering sections: Cash Flows from Operating Activities, Cash Flows from Investing Activities, and Cash Flows from Financing Activities. Within each section, some of the entries are difficult to understand because they do not flow in a consistent manner from the Balance Sheet and Income Statement and others are simply incomprehensible. I believe the standard Generally Accepted Accounting Principles (GAAP) format for Cash Flow was devised to keep Chief Executive Officers in their place.

The presentation of Cash Flow in the Operational Plan will stand the scrutiny of professional investors but is understandable and useful. In the Cash Flow, the financial activities of the company are divided into Sources and Uses of cash. Since all financial activities can either increase or decrease the amount of cash available to a business, the assignment of an activity to the Source or the Use category is somewhat arbitrary. This presentation defines Sources as Net Earnings, Depreciation, increase in Accounts Payable, and Sale of Equity; and defines Uses as increase in Accounts Receivable, increase in Raw Materials, increase in Finished Goods, and Purchase of Capital Assets.

- Sources:

  ○ Net Earnings generate cash and are the starting point of this exercise.

  ○ Depreciation generates cash because on the Income Statement it was listed as an expense and therefore reduced Earnings, but since no actual cash was paid out during the period, we still have that cash.

  ○ An increase in Accounts Payable generates cash because an increase in what you owe to your suppliers is cash you did not pay out of your bank account. Think of it this way: when you charge a purchase to your credit card instead of paying cash, you will have more cash in your pocket.

  ○ The Sale of Equity generates new cash. In the example, New Products Corporation sells $950,000 in equity during July. This represents the net venture capital investment after deducting expenses.

- Uses:

  ○ An increase in Accounts Receivable reduces the amount of cash because the total amount of cash collected from customers is less than purchases by customers. If one friend repays a $25 loan and another borrows $50, you have less cash in your pocket because your receivables have increased.

  ○ An increase in inventory, either Raw Materials or

Finished Goods, reduces the amount of cash because the inventory costs money. This can be a difficult concept to comprehend because it is essentially an adjustment to a timing issue, namely that the Income Statement "recognizes" Earnings based on the timing of the sale regardless when the material itself was purchased. I asked my daughter Lenore, a management consultant, for her explanation. She said, "Isn't it more about the matching? If you buy $100 worth of materials in one month and use them in the next, the money is recognized as an expense in the second month to match it to the sale, but the flow of cash actually went out the month before, so this is why you need the adjustment." Whatever line of reasoning may be best for you, an increase in inventory reduces cash.

o   And finally, the Purchase of Capital Assets reduces cash. Some long-ago entrepreneur offered the following advice about Capital Assets, "Never purchase what you can lease, never lease what you can rent, never rent what you can borrow, and never borrow what you can steal." Sounds like pretty good advice.

Two of the eight entries under Cash Flow (Net Earnings and Depreciation) are items from the Income Statement. The remaining six entries are changes to Balance Sheet accounts and, in the forecast period, these six entries are assumptions. The estimates and formulas you enter as assumptions reflect the operational priorities of the company. In the example, the formula to calculate the month-to-month increase in Accounts Payable assumes the current month's Accounts Payable consists of the amount of Raw Materials consumed in the current plus the previous month. This is a pretty good starting point, but you need to build formulas into your spreadsheet that reflect the

Accounts Payable and Accounts Receivable cycles of your company as accurately as possible.

The final part of the Operational Plan is the Balance Sheet. The Actual columns of the Balance Sheet are obtained from the usual outputs of the company's accounting system. These entries are easy to understand and, in the event your accounting system does not automatically generate the item, easy to manually calculate.

- Bank is the amount of cash the company would have if there were no outstanding checks or deposits. Start with the month-end bank statement: deduct outstanding checks (those written during the month but not yet recorded by the bank) and add outstanding deposits and credits (those made or taken during the month but not yet recorded by the bank).
- Accounts Receivable is the total amount owed to the company by its customers at the end of the month.
- Raw Materials are the total cost of Raw Materials in inventory.
- Finished Goods are the total cost, Raw Materials plus Direct Labor, of Finished Goods in inventory.
- Capital Assets are the total cost of the furniture, equipment, computers and other property belonging to the company, minus accumulated Depreciation.
- Accounts Payable is the total amount owed by the company to its suppliers at the end of the month.
- Capital Stock is the total amount shareholders' have paid for their shares.
- Retained Earnings are the accumulated Earnings, or loss, of the company since the beginning of time.

The Balance Sheet is an embodiment of the philosophical concept that a company is an entity in perfect balance. What the company owns, its Assets, are exactly balanced by what the company owes, its Liabilities. This fact will be useful in checking the data, formulas and assumptions for forecast periods. The Balance Sheet, which is generated by the spreadsheet program in the forecast period, will not balance until all the numbers and formulas you have entered are in the correct form.

INDEX

I

J

K

L

M

Printed in the United States
39475LVS00002B/88-90